MY NOTES ON HINDU PHILOSOPHY

An insatiable quest

CHANDRASHEKHAR CHAUBEY

BlueRoseONE.com
Stories Matter
NewDelhi • London

BLUEROSE PUBLISHERS
India | U.K.

BlueRose ONE
Stories Matter
NewDelhi • London

For permissions requests or inquiries regarding this publication, please contact:

BLUEROSE PUBLISHERS
www.BlueRoseONE.com
info@bluerosepublishers.com
+91 8882 898 898
+4407342408967

ISBN: 978-93-7310-198-9

Cover Design: Aman Sharma
Typesetting: Pooja Sharma

First Edition: September 2025

To my parents, mother late *Kamla Chaubey*, father late *Narmdeshwar Chaubey* and my guru *Bhramleen swani Vidyanand Giri ji Maharaj* (10th *Maha mandleshwar of Kailash ashram Rishikesh*), for initiating spiritual thoughts in my formative years

PREFACE

Atho bharman Jigyasa (now there is a curiosity to know brahman or creator), is the opening phrase of *Bhrahmsutra*, which aptly applies to me, by virtue of being born and brought up in orthodox *hindu* family at *Rishikesh* (town in Uttrakhand) where *hindu* ritualistic traditions, philosophical studies and practices are the part of everyday life, my formative years brought seeds of *hindu* spirituality in me and it remained dormant as I moved ahead in material world, after completing studies and then to drudgery of life in job for living, marriage, family and children, now having passed midlife and kids moving to college, things around me slowed down and seed of spirituality found a fertile ground, but curiosity needs direction to learning and to undertake quest in understanding myself, which appeared morbid initially, as it involves individual soul (*atman*), supreme soul (brahman), our state in waking, dreaming and sleep without dream, however as studies moved, I realized that it is all intuitive in everyday life and it helped me understand more clearly to myself and things around me.

Lot of time was spent in structuring studies that needs to be undertaken, and help came from revered sages in *ashram* (hermitrage) where I used to go in childhood with my parents, and by seeking direction from them and turning pages of suggested text by them and with the transcendental grace, I could get direction to begin my studies of *hindu* spiritual text in *vedic* system, and study of spiritual text was never satisfying and each time I tried to understand, further intriguing it became and it is insatiable quest now, where each of aphorism in any of the philosophical text gets a fresh perspective of understanding when heard or read from different revered people.

As my studies continued by reading and listening to sages on explanations of subjects and topics, I kept my notes and marginalia and, in this compilation, I tried to stitch my notes together, however it is extremely vast and deep that each of the thought in text takes lifetime to fully understand, practice and to perfect it, which may not be possible unless one has transcendental blessings and guru to guide to make spiritual progress in this life and creating seed (*samskara*) for many life to come.

Six different philosophies authored at different timeline are considered pillars of the *hindu* philosophy which finds it base in four *vedas* which is considered primordial of origin and has authority from *brahman* (creator or supreme self) itself and is unchallenged, each of the four *vedas* that is *Samveda, Yajurveds, Arthaveda* and *Rigveda* is divided in four sections of *Samhita, Brahmanas, Arayanaks* and *Upnishads* where first two are ritualistic part of *vedas* and *Arayanaks* are partially philosophical when persons moves to forest at later part of life with limited resources whereas *Upnishads* are entirely philosophical, *Vedas* conveys four supreme goals in one's life, which are known as *Purusharthas* and it's guiding principles to all are *Dharma* – it pertains to living virtuous life aligned with responsibilities and societal norms, emphasizing righteousness, duty, and ethical conduct, *Artha* - representing pursuit of legitimate means to achieve material prosperity, wealth, and success, focusing on economic well-being and fulfilling one's material needs, *Kama* - pursuit of aesthetic, emotional, and sensual pleasures in life, encompassing desires, sensual enjoyment, love, art, relationships and *Moksha*- aim of spiritual liberation, seeking freedom from the cycle of birth and rebirth (*samsara*), aiming for union with the divine, realization of the true self (*Atman*), and understanding the ultimate cosmic reality (*Brahman*).

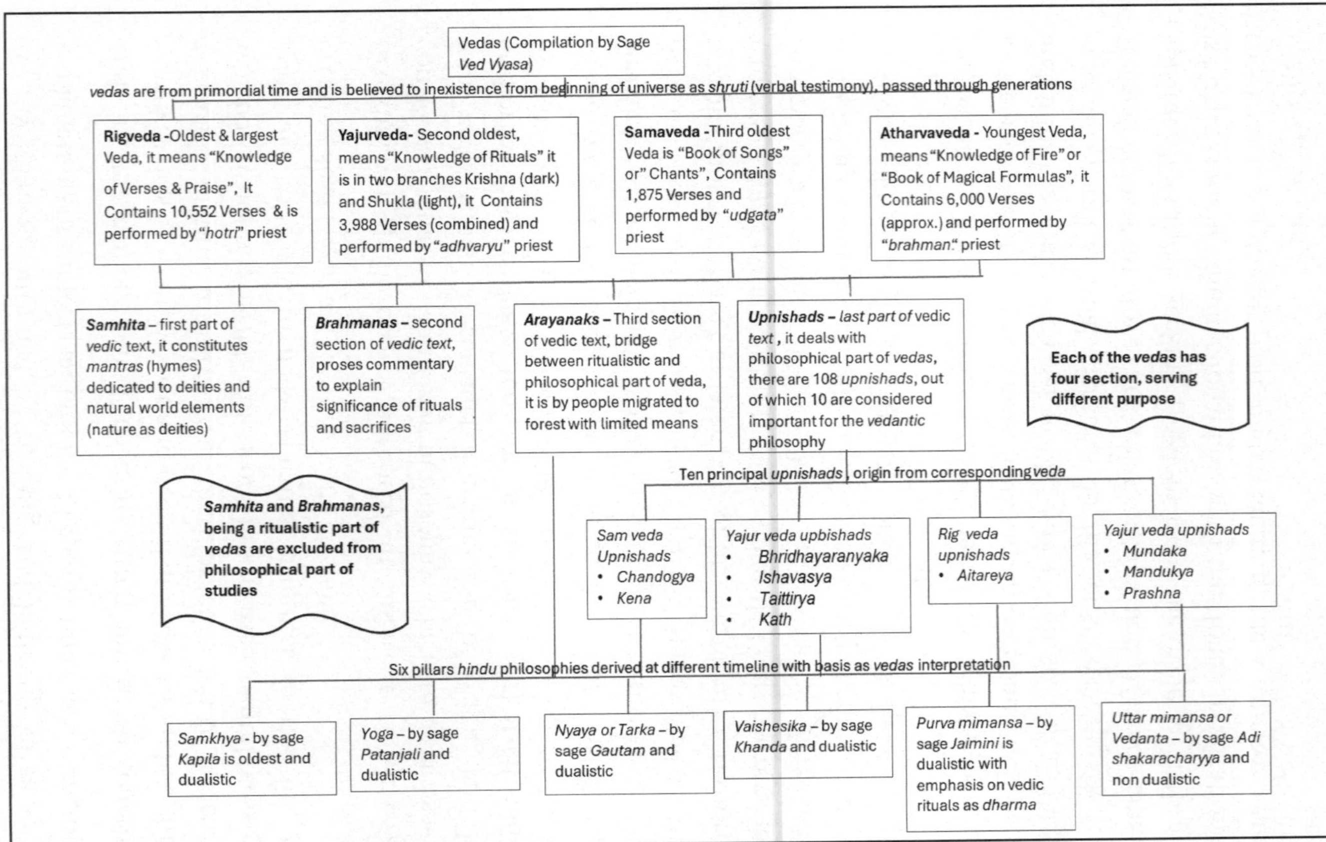
Vedas (Compilation by Sage Ved Vyasa)
vedas are from primordial time and is believed to inexistence from beginning of universe as shruti (verbal testimony), passed through generations
Rigveda -Oldest & largest Veda, it means "Knowledge of Verses & Praise", It Contains 10,552 Verses & is performed by "hotri" priest
Yajurveda- Second oldest, means "Knowledge of Rituals" it is in two branches Krishna (dark) and Shukla (light), it Contains 3,988 Verses (combined) and performed by "adhvaryu" priest
Samaveda -Third oldest Veda is "Book of Songs" or" Chants", Contains 1,875 Verses and performed by "udgata" priest
Atharvaveda - Youngest Veda, means "Knowledge of Fire" or "Book of Magical Formulas", it Contains 6,000 Verses (approx.) and performed by "brahman" priest
Samhita – first part of vedic text, it constitutes mantras (hymes) dedicated to deities and natural world elements (nature as deities)
Brahmanas – second section of vedic text, proses commentary to explain significance of rituals and sacrifices
Arayanaks – Third section of vedic text, bridge between ritualistic and philosophical part of veda, it is by people migrated to forest with limited means
Upnishads – last part of vedic text, it deals with philosophical part of vedas, there are 108 upnishads, out of which 10 are considered important for the vedantic philosophy
Each of the vedas has four section, serving different purpose
Samhita and Brahmanas, being a ritualistic part of vedas are excluded from philosophical part of studies
Ten principal upnishads, origin from corresponding veda
Sam veda Upnishads
• Chandogya
• Kena
Yajur veda upbishads
• Bhridhayaranyaka
• Ishavasya
• Taittirya
• Kath
Rig veda upnishads
• Aitareya
Yajur veda upnishads
• Mundaka
• Mandukya
• Prashna
Six pillars hindu philosophies derived at different timeline with basis as vedas interpretation
Samkhya - by sage Kapila is oldest and dualistic
Yoga – by sage Patanjali and dualistic
Nyaya or Tarka – by sage Gautam and dualistic
Vaishesika – by sage Khanda and dualistic
Purva mimansa – by sage Jaimini is dualistic with emphasis on vedic rituals as dharma
Uttar mimansa or Vedanta – by sage Adi shakaracharyya and non dualistic

Six philosophies *Shankhya, Yoga, Nyaya (tarka), Viseshika, purva-mimansa* and *Upnishids* each takes different point of view from dualistic to monism and need of deity to atheist to pure *brahman* and rest all being its manifestation however except *Upnishad or vedantic* philosophy rest all are silent on creation, however all of it takes common point of need for liberation of the human from the present state and provide road map to liberation.

Samkhya philosophy by sage *Kapila* is oldest philosophy believed to be developed around 550 BCE, it is dualistic philosophy focusing on the interaction of consciousness (*Purusha*) and nature (*Prakriti*), It explores the evolution of the universe from *Prakriti* (nature), which is initially in a state of equilibrium or unmanifested and evolve world through the interaction of the three *gunas* (qualities) to twenty four *padartahs* (elements). *Yogasutra* by sage *Patanjali* is believed to be developed around 200 BCE, it is dualistic but practical philosophy emphasizing meditation, contemplation, and self-control to achieve liberation *(moksha)*, It is closely related to *Samkhya* and often studied together, it emphasizes the path of self-realization through practices of meditation, aiming for liberation *(moksha)*, God or *Isvara*, is viewed as a special, supreme Self, untouched by suffering, *karma* and its effects, and is considered the source of all knowledge and the guide to spiritual liberation, where liberation is realization of self.

Nyaya or Tarka philosophy by sage *Akṣapada Gautama* is believed to be developed around 600 BCE to 200 CE, it is a dualistic school of logic and epistemology that explores the sources of knowledge by valid reasoning and emphasizing importance of valid reasoning and arguments with six *pramanas* or means of knowledge, where God is conceived as the efficient cause of the universe, creator, sustainer, and destroyer, possessing attributes of omniscience, omnipresence, and infinite perfections, but not the material cause, which is considered to be eternal atoms and liberation or *Moksha* is the ultimate goal, representing freedom from suffering and the cycle of birth and death, achieved through attaining true knowledge and disassociating self from body and sense organs.

Vaisheshika by sage *Kaṇada Kashyapa* also known as *Uluka* is believed to be developed around 200-300 CE is a dualistic and empiricist philosophy that focuses on the atomic nature of reality and the categories of existence, it explores nature of reality, emphasizing the existence of atoms and their combinations, it is closely related to *Nyaya* philosophy and often studied together and, it considers four *pramanas* or means of knowledge while God is not explicitly named but divine or God is understood as the ultimate cause of the creation, maintenance, and destruction of the universe, supervising the actions of atoms and souls according to the law of *karma* and liberation or *moksha* is achieved through attaining correct knowledge of reality, which allows individual soul to escape cycle of suffering and bondage caused by ignorance.

Purva Mimamsa or *Mimamsa* by sage *Jaimini* is believed to be developed around 400 BCE, it focuses on interpretation and understanding of the *Vedas,* particularly the rituals and actions prescribed within it, emphasizing the importance of *dharma* (duty) and *vedas* being only valid source to know *dharma* or duty, it Is not a pure theistic philosophy but focus is on the *vedic* rituals and their efficacy, rather than concept of a supreme being, while acknowledging the existence of *vedic* deities, it emphasizes importance of performing rituals correctly to achieve desired outcomes but not by worshipping or seeking boons from these deities, liberation in *Mimansa* emphasizes the idea of *svarga* or heavenly abode and *apurva* or unseen results generated through by fulfilment of one's duties or *dharma,* leading to positive *karma* and eventually leading to liberation from the cycle of birth and death.

Vedanta, or Uttara Mimamsa, has roots in the Vedic period roughly 1500-500 BCE and developed further through various schools and

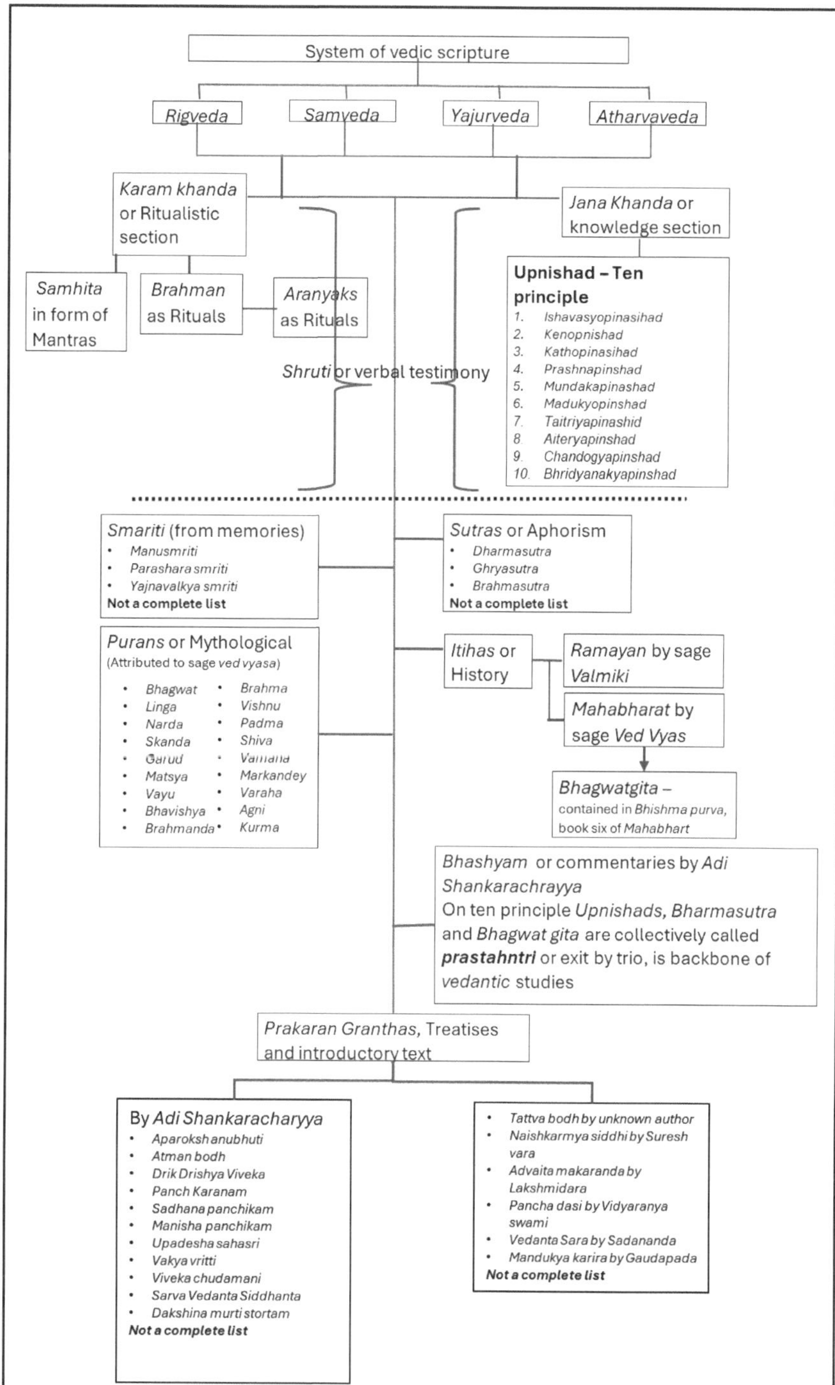
System of vedic scripture
Rigveda
Samveda
Yajurveda
Atharvaveda
Karam khanda or Ritualistic section
Jana Khanda or knowledge section
Samhita in form of Mantras
Brahman as Rituals
Aranyaks as Rituals
Shruti or verbal testimony
Upnishad – Ten principle
1. Ishavasyopinasihad
2. Kenopnishad
3. Kathopinasihad
4. Prashnapinshad
5. Mundakapinashad
6. Madukyopinshad
7. Taitriyapinashid
8. Aiteryapinshad
9. Chandogyapinshad
10. Bhridyanakyapinshad
Smariti (from memories)
Manusmriti
Parashara smriti
Yajnavalkya smriti
Not a complete list
Sutras or Aphorism
Dharmasutra
Ghryasutra
Brahmasutra
Not a complete list
Purans or Mythological
(Attributed to sage ved vyasa)
Bhagwat
Brahma
Linga
Vishnu
Narda
Padma
Skanda
Shiva
Garud
Vamana
Matsya
Markandey
Vayu
Varaha
Bhavishya
Agni
Brahmanda
Kurma
Itihas or History
Ramayan by sage Valmiki
Mahabharat by sage Ved Vyas
Bhagwatgita – contained in Bhishma purva, book six of Mahabhart
Bhashyam or commentaries by Adi Shankarachrayya
On ten principle Upnishads, Bharmasutra and Bhagwat gita are collectively called prastahntri or exit by trio, is backbone of vedantic studies
Prakaran Granthas, Treatises and introductory text
By Adi Shankaracharyya
Aparoksh anubhuti
Atman bodh
Drik Drishya Viveka
Panch Karanam
Sadhana panchikam
Manisha panchikam
Upadesha sahasri
Vakya vritti
Viveka chudamani
Sarva Vedanta Siddhanta
Dakshina murti stortam
Not a complete list
Tattva bodh by unknown author
Naishkarmya siddhi by Suresh vara
Advaita makaranda by Lakshmidara
Pancha dasi by Vidyaranya swami
Vedanta Sara by Sadananda
Mandukya karira by Gaudapada
Not a complete list

thinkers, majorly by *Adi Shankara*char*yya* in 800 CE shaping *Advaita Vedanta,* it is a non-dualistic philosophy which focuses teachings of the *Upanishads* which is mystic or spiritual contemplations within the *Vedas,* three main components are defined with first as *Brahman or Ishvara* or supreme self which is the ultimate reality, second is *Atman* or the individual souls and third is the *Prakriti* or the physical world. When it comes to the relationship between the three it says Brahman and *Atman* are one and the same and

Brahman is the material and efficient cause of *prakrirti.* Later much of the work was done by *Madhvacharya* (dualism), *Ramanujacharya* (qualified dualism) etc. where God is understood as *Brahman* described as beyond human comprehension, formless, and without attributes, existing as pure existence, consciousness, and bliss (*Sat-Chit-Ananda*), the ultimate, impersonal, and transcendent reality, which is underlying principle of all existence, liberation (*Moksha or Mukti)* signifies freedom from the cycle of birth and death (*Samsara*) and the attainment of self-realization, achieved through the realization of one's true nature as *Brahman,* the ultimate reality.

Vedantic studies encompasses three text which are collectively called as *prasthantri* or exit with trio with first as ten principal *upnishads* which are philosophical part of *vedas* as *smriti prasthan* or derived from memories of revered sages, second being *Bhagwat gita or Gita* which *shruti prastan* or testimony by God himself are often referred as another *upnishad* and third being *Bhramsutra* as *tarka prasthan* or logic, it synthesises works of all *upnishads* developed at various timeline and logically brings harmony among contradictions in them along with refutation of all other philosophies against the *vedantic* philosophy.

Table of Contents

SANKHYA PHILOSOPHY 1

YOGA PHILOSOPHY 5

NYAYA PHILOSOPHY 18

VAISHESHIKA PHILOSOPHY 31

PURVA MIMANSA 38

VEDANTA/ PRASTANTRI 44

BHAGWATGITA 46

UPNISHAD 76

AITAREYA- Master Aitarey 78

BRIHADARANYAKA - Discussion in Forest 82

CHANDOGYA - Keys of Knowledge 109

ISHAVASYA- The Lord 113

KENAO – At Whose Command 115

KATHO - Kathak Branch of Veda 117

TAITTIRYA – Taittirya Branch of Veda 123

MUNDAKA– In the Feet of Monk 130

PRASHNA – Questions, Elaboration of Mundka Upnishad 136

MANDUKYA – Master Mandukya 141

BHRAMSUTRA 144

SANKHYA PHILOSOPHY

Sankhya (literally means count, enumerate or empirical) is a dualistic philosophy, It views reality as composed of two independent entities, *Puruṣa* or *Bhokta* (consciousness and passive enjoyer) and *Prakṛti* or *Bhogya* (nature or matter, including the human mind and emotions or subject to be enjoyed)

Puruṣa being witness and pure consciousness and is absolute, independent, free, beyond perception, above any experience by mind or senses, and impossible to describe in words.

Prakriti is a matter or nature, it is inactive, unconscious, and is at balance of the three *guṇas* (qualities or innate tendencies), namely *sattva*(poise, joy), *rajas*(dynamism, impelling),and *tamas*(inertia, sloth).

When *Prakṛti* comes into contact with *Purusha* this balance is disturbed, and *Prakriti* becomes manifested, evolving twenty-three *tattvas* (elements), which are intellect (*buddhi, mahat*), self - conscious or ego (*ahamkara*), mind (*manas*), five sensory capacities (ears, skin, eyes, tongue and nose), five action capacities (hands (hasta), feet (pada), speech (vak), anus (*guda*), and genitals (*upastha*)) and five "subtle elements" or "modes of sensory content" (*tanmatras*), from which the five "gross elements" emerges which are perceptual objects (earth, water, fire, air and (ether) space), which in turn giving rise to sensory experience and cognition of the manifestation.

Thought processes and mental events are conscious only to the extent they receive illumination from *Purusha,* where consciousness is compared to light which illuminates the material configurations or 'shapes' assumed by the mind. Hence, intellect after receiving cognitive structures from the mind and illumination from pure consciousness, creates thought structures that appear to be conscious and *Ahamkara* (self-consciousness), the ego appropriates all mental experiences to itself and personalizes the objective activities of mind through intellect by assuming possession of it, but consciousness itself is independent of the thought structures it illuminates, like sun illuminating all, remains independent of objects it illuminates.

Jiva (individual soul) is said to be in the state where *Puruṣa* is bonded to *Prakriti* and human experience is an interplay of the two, *Puruṣa* being conscious of the various combinations of cognitive activities, and at the end of the bondage of *Puruṣa* to *Prakriti* is called *Moksha* (Liberation) or *Kaivalya* (Isolation), whereas *Jiva* has natural quest for *moksha* (liberation).

Puruṣa is the eternal pure consciousness, but due to ignorance, it identifies itself with products of *Prakṛti* such as intellect *(buddhi)* and ego (*ahamkara*) which is the causes of bondage and sufferings (*samsara*) and it results in endless transmigration and suffering, however way out of this suffering is through knowledge (*viveka*), and by knowing difference between *Prakṛti* (*avyakta-vyakta*) and *Puruṣa* and, once this realization arises that *Puruṣa* is distinct from *Prakṛti*, which is more than empirical ego and that *puruṣa* is in deepest conscious self within, by knowing this oneself gains isolation (*kaivalya*) and freedom (*moksha*).

Sankhya accepts three of six *pramaṇas* ('proofs') as the only reliable means of gaining knowledge, these are *pratyakṣa* ('perception'), *anumaṇa* ('inference') and *sabda* (*aptavacana*, meaning, 'word/testimony of reliable sources'), and it is one of the most rational philosophy, which relies exclusively on reason.

The *Sankhya* system is based on *Sat-karya-vada* or the theory of causation, where effect is pre-existent in cause and there is only an illusory change in the makeup of the cause and not a material one when cause becomes effect, since effects cannot come from nothing, hence the primary cause or ground of everything is seen as *Prakṛti.*

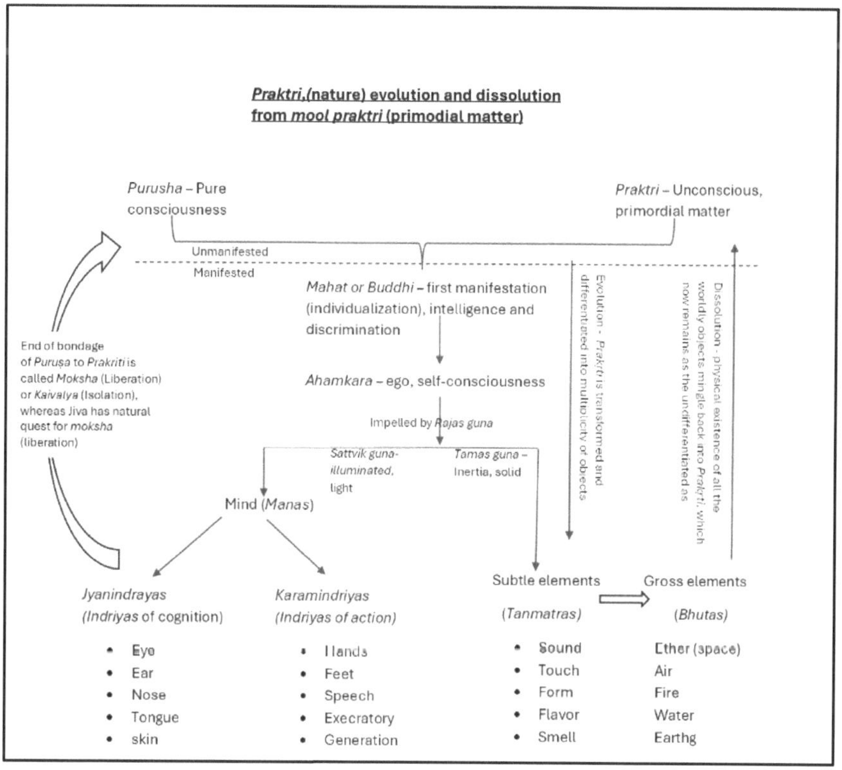

Cause under consideration is *Prakṛti* or more precisely *Mool-Prakṛti* ("Primordial Matter"), hence *Samkhya* system is an exponent of an evolutionary theory of matter beginning with primordial matter, where during evolution, *Prakṛti* is transformed and differentiated into multiplicity of objects and in the same way as evolution it is followed up by dissolution, during dissolution physical existence of all the worldly objects reverts back into *Prakṛti*, where all physical existence remains undifferentiated as primordial substance. This is how the cycles of evolution and dissolution follow each other, uniqueness of *Samkhya* is that not only physical entities but even mind, ego and intelligence are regarded as forms of unconsciousness which emerges and dissolves in *praktri,* which is distinct from pure consciousness or *purusha.*

Evolution is possible because *Prakṛti* is always in a state of tension among its constituent *gunas – sattva, rajas* and *tamas* and are in state of equilibrium, and all three together are one unmanifest" *Prakṛti* which is unknowable since it is unmanifested, but when *guṇa* in the unified entity changes, either by increase or decrease of any one or all *gunas* manifestation occurs, for this reason pure consciousness is called *nirguna* or without any modification since all modifications happen to *praktri* but not to *purusha.*

This evolution obeys causality relationships, with primal nature being the material cause of all physical creation where cause and effect theory of *Samkhya* is called *Sat-karya-vada* ("theory of existent causes"), and holds that nothing can really be created from or destroyed into nothingness and all evolution is simply the transformation of primal nature from one form to another.

Sankhya is atheistic philosophy, but with its classical systematization in which existence of a deity became irrelevant.

YOGA PHILOSOPHY

Genre of *Yoga & Sankhya* philosophy is dualism; both considers consciousness and matter or self/soul and body as two different realities. *Yoga* philosophy differs from the closely related *sankhya* philosophy by incorporating the concept of a personal, yet essentially inactive deity or personal god (*Ishvara*), however both *sankhya* and *yoga* philosophy avoids question on creation. Two independent realities are *Purusha* and *Prakriti*, While *Prakriti* is a single entity, but *Sankhya & Yoga* philosophy admit a plurality of the *Puruṣa*s in this world, *Prakriti* alone is the only source of the world of objects and material creation.

Puruṣa is considered as pure consciousness and a passive enjoyer (*bhokta*), while *Prakriti* is the enjoyed (*bhogya*), *Samkhya* and *Yoga* philosophy believes that the *Puruṣa* cannot be regarded as the source of insentient world, because an intelligent thing cannot transform itself into the unconscious world, hence it is a pluralistic spiritualism with many souls, but have reality built on the foundation of dualism.

Yoga philosophy adopts theory of *guna* from *Sankhya*, as three *gunas* (innate tendency or attributes) are present in different proportions in all beings, and these three are *sattva guna* (goodness or constructive or harmonious), *rajas guna* (passion or activity or confused), and *tamas guna* (darkness or destructive or chaotic). These three *gunas* are present in every being in different proportions, and the fundamental nature and psychological dispositions of beings is a consequence of their relative proportion of these three *gunas*. When *sattva guna* predominates in an individual then quality of lucidity, wisdom, constructiveness, harmonious, and peacefulness manifest within themselves, when *rajas guna* is predominant then , attachment, craving, passion-driven activity and restlessness manifest within that person and when *tamas guna* predominates in an individual then ignorance, delusion, destructive, lethargy, and suffering manifests within that person, this *guans* theory underpins philosophy of mind in *Yoga* philosophy.

According to *yoga* philosophy, *Puruṣa* (consciousness) by its natural nature is *sattva* (constructive), while *Prakriti* (matter) by its innate nature is *tamas* (chaotic), this is the reason when an individuals at birth have *buddhi* (intelligence) which is *sattvic,* as life progresses and churns one's *buddhi,* it creates *asmita* or *ahamkara* (ego or self-consciousness) which is *rajasic* and when ego in turn is churned by life then *manas* (temper, mood) are transformed to *tamasic.*

Interaction of *buddhi* (intellect), *ahamkara* (ego or self-consciousness) and *manas* (Mind) are collective constituent of *citta* (mind stuff) in *Yoga* philosophy and modification of *citta* causes suffering, however leading to a way of life that empowers one to

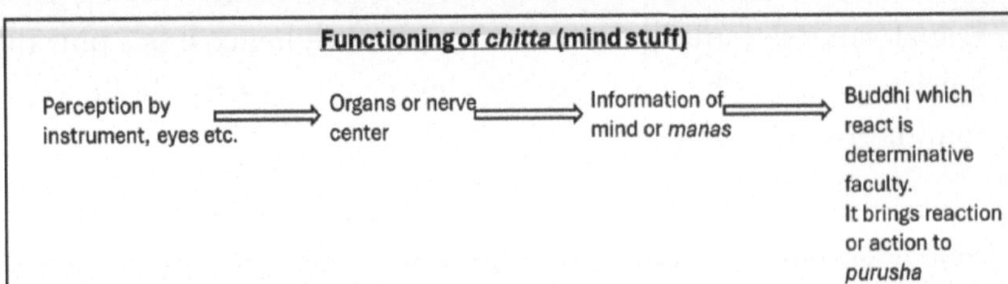

become ever more aware of one's consciousness and spirituality innate in *buddhi* (Intellect), is the path to one's highest potential and a more serene, content, liberated life. *Patanjali's Yoga sutra* begins, defining Yoga as "restraining the *Citta* from *Vrittis* "(whirlpool of thoughts).

Vritti is waves of thought or force arising, when external causes impinge on self, it can be visualized as lake is *chitta* and ripples or wave on surface is *vritti,* our true self is bottom of the lake and due to muddy and agitated water due to ripples or wave one does not see bottom of the lake or cannot see their true self.

Chitta is always trying to get back to its natural pure state, but organs draw it out based on state of mind (*manas*), covered by three *gunas, tamas* (dull form) which is demonical and inclined to hurt others are said to be active

state, rajas (scattered form) which is devas (God) and gives motive for power and for enjoyment, sattva (*ekagra chitta*) which is *samadhi* (deep meditation), serenity and calmness and is active state.

Yog sutra, is guiding script by sage *Patanjali* on *yoga* philosophy, it has 195 aphorisms divided in four chapters

Samadhai pada **(enlightenment through meditation)** – *Samadhai* or deep meditation is a blissful state of yogi, where he is absorbed in nature (*praktri*), but there is not liberation from rebirth since seeds of actions are not destroyed, where *Samsara* (impressions) are large in number for soul and it comes from repeated actions that are forming habits, and when habits are repeated it forms character, however *vairagya* (dispassion) are achieved by two fold motive, first by power by controlling own experiences and another one is from others experiences.

Prana or vital breath is not the breathing alone but is considered as energy of universe, later *yogis* has defined *Ida* (left spinal column) and *Pingla* (right spinal column) which takes current for the function of life and the third one *Susumna* (middle spinal column) is a vacant channel and it works for *yogi* only.

Types of *Samadhai* (deep meditation)

<table>
<tr>
<td>Samprajnta samadhi – it is with higher knowledge, which occurs through the absorption of the mind into an object of meditation, and as the samskara (impressions) is not destroyed, it is considered Savikalpa, which has four stages, each maturating to another level

1. Savitkara – meditate on gross objects (twenty-four elements) on their nature with relation to time and space

2. Savichara – meditate on subtle elements or tanmatras on their nature in relation to time and space, it can be with or without discrimination of self to object

3. Sananda – giving up gross and subtle elements and meditate on sattvik mind only

4. Asmita – meditate on sattvik ego only, which leads to prakrtilya that is merged in praktri or nature</td>
<td>Asamprajnata samadhi – it is beyond higher knowledge, there is no object of concentration, rather yogi's consciousness is merged with supreme consciousness and all samskara or impressions are destroyed, this state is like ocean with no waves.

This the only sadhana (practice) for attaining state of Para Vairagya, where rajas and tamas are destroyed and It is the only means of obtaining kavaliya / moksha or liberation.</td>
</tr>
</table>

Various forms of meditation

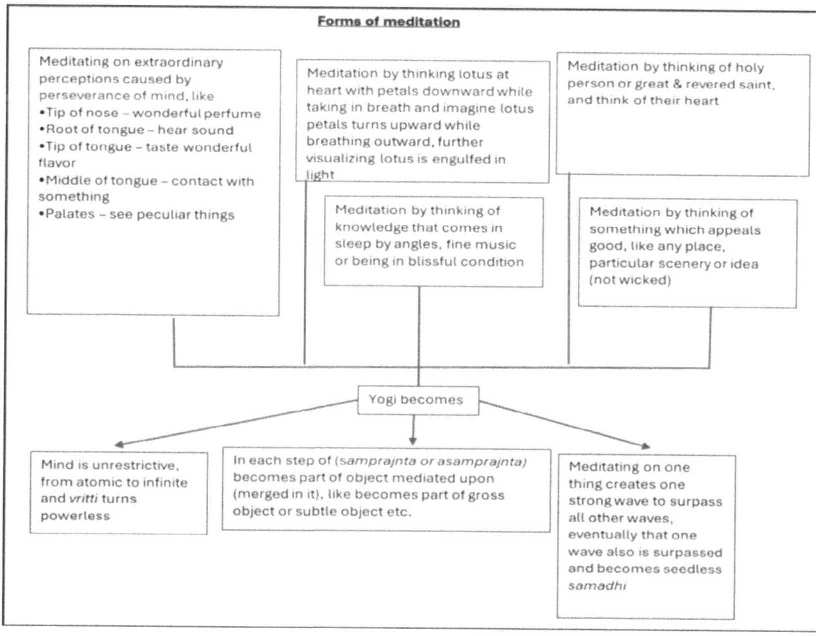

***Sadhana* pada – concentration / practice –** it defines two stream of yoga practice, which are *Kriya yoga* and *Astang yoga*

Kriya yoga – emphasis is on factors of modification, study and fruit of action surrendering to God, it elaborates that modification is by controlling of *indriyas* (senses) and by study till all confusion and conflict are resolved and then eventually surrendering all fruits of action by which there is no credit or blame for the action and one is at peace.

However, obstructions in attaining this state and suggested mitigation for it and the final state are

Obstructions	Means of destruction of ignorance is by practice of discrimination of *purusa* (consciousness) and *priktri* (nature)	Mitigation
•Ignorance – considering body as man and is a delusion •Egoism – identifying ourselves as self and thinking that it cannot change •Attachments – in the hope of pleasure •Aversion – trying to pre-empt pain •Clinging – flowing through in its own nature		•Controlling *samskara* – by opposite modification, to reject negative thoughts by opposite thoughts •All works in present are the fruits of *samskara*, and it will manifest again as future action •Suffering of misery not yet manifested, can be avoided at the junction of *purusha* (consciousness) and *nature* (mind)

Outcome of practice of discrimination of *praktri* and *purusha* is

- Satisfaction and cessation of seeking knowledge here and there and realizing it is within us
- All physical and mental pain vanishes with attainment of knowledge
- Attains complete knowledge of omniscience and realizing that it is within us
- Freedom of *chitta* (mind stuff) from difficulties and struggle fallen from us and *chitta* melts away to cause
- Person is established in its own soul, that they are alone through the universe.

Person established in *Kriya yoga* acts as witness only, where neither body or mind is connected to him, and they are working on their own way and we through ignorance are joined to it.

Astang yoga* or eight limbs of *yoga – It is step by step guide which eventually leads to moksha or liberation, this stream of yoga defines eight consecutive steps to be practiced for attaining liberation, where first five steps as practicing restraint on external things and later three steps on practicing restraint on internal activity

External restraint practice

1. *Yama* – non killing of others (*ahinsa*), truthfulness with self and others, practicing continence and non-receiving from others
2. *Niyam* – Internal and external purification, containment of thoughts and actions, restraining mortification to others, study of prescribed literature and worship of God
3. *Asana* – practicing firm and pleasant posture of body
4. *Pranayama* – controlling of inhalation and exhalation of *prana* or vital breath, which is considered not a breath alone but is sum total of cosmic energies.
    a. It results in awakening of *kundli,* which are seven spiritual energy centres in body or *chakras*
    b. Removes rajas and tamas, which covers *chitta* and prepares one for next step
5. *Prathyara* – Drawing all senses inward and insulating oneself from outside

> *Kundali or Chakras* or energy centers in body
>
> 1. *Mooladhara* - beneath spinal cord
> 2. Swadisthan – at abdomen area
> 3. *Manipura* – at navel area
> 4. *Anahata* – at heart
> 5. *Vishuddha* – at throat
> 6. *Ajna* – forehead or third eye
> 7. *Sahasrara* – at crown of head

Internal restraint practice

6. *Dharna* – Holding mind on single object
7. *Dhyan* – concentrating on *guna* (qualities) of object with unbroken flow of knowledge of that object

8. *Samadhai* – Being with oneness with self

Internal restraints are also known as *samyana,* which is highest order of meditation leading to *moksha/ kavilya* or liberation.

Vibhooti pada (**power attained by *****yoga*****)** – *Dharana* is holding the mind on to some object with uninterrupted flow (of the mind) towards the object chosen for meditation and by this contemplation, *yogi* forget himself and unite with the object of *dhyana* (meditation) and this state is known as *samadhi.*

Three (*dharana, dhyana, samadhi*) together on same object Is called *samyama* by mastering on *sanyama, prajna* (light of higher consciousness) comes & that (*sanyama*) should be applied in different *bhoomis* (stages) one after another, this group of three (*dharana, dhyana, and samadhi*) is the inner limb distinct from the previous five limbs of yoga, but even they (*dharana,dhyana* and *samadhi*) are *nirbeeja* - the seedless samadhi where *samskara* (impression) are not destroyed.

During the state of *nirodha* where the mind is calm and free from excessive mental activity and at the state of *vyutthan* where mind is at active state and thoughts are arising with mental modifications happening, so in both state, *sanskars* are effective but when in *nirodha* state (in which *sanskars* are suppressed), where due to influence of this *nirodh samskara,* which leads to state of mind to the yogi which is completely calm.

Samadhi (deep meditation) transformation is gradual setting from distractions and rising to the single-pointedness, in *samadhi* (in the state of deep concentration) past and present modifications are similar, it is *ekagrata-parinama* or mutation of the stabilised state of mind, as a results of restraint, *samadhi* or concentration of mind is elaborated earlier, where transformation of the visible characteristics, time factors and conditions of elements and senses are also described in that section

By performing Samyama

- on the sound - comprehension of the meaning of sounds uttered by any living being
- on latent impressions - one obtains knowledge of one's past lives.
- *on chitta* of another man - one obtains knowledge of the nature of his mind.
- on his own body - connection between the eye and the light get obstructed of other person and due to this that person is not able to see the body of the Yogi consequently the body of a Yogi is invisible.
- on *karmas* or inauspicious signs - Yogi gets fore knowledge of death.

  on *maitri* (friendliness), *karuna* (Compassion)- one can develops power in all these.
- on physical strength- strength of elephants etc. can be acquired.
- on effulgent light of higher sense- knowledge of subtle objects, or things obstructed from view, or at a great distance, can be acquired.
- on the sun- one gains knowledge of the cosmic spaces.
- on the moon- one gains knowledge of the arrangement of the stars.
- on polestar- one gains knowledge of the motions of the stars.
- on navel plexus- knowledge of the body's constitution
- on the hollow of the throat- one can be free from hunger and thirst.
- on *koorma nadi* (energy channel located in throat region)- one becomes steady.
- on light at crown of the head- one gets a vision of the perfected beings.
- on the heart- knowledge of the mind-stuff is obtained.

Dharmi is referred as inherent property or characteristics which is underlying reality that remains constant in past, present and future despite the transformations of *dharma* (nature), *lakshana* (characteristics), and *Avastha* (state), hence change of sequence (of characteristics) is the cause of manifold evolution like lump of clay when grinded is dirt and when soaked in water is slush is the change of sequence to *dharmi* (clay) so as with external restraint one gets evolved in in better robust and flexible body and with internal restraint one start getting improved results, and as the practice matures and power gained by studying characteristics and state of any object simultaneously in *samyana*, in this way, *yogi* gets kind of power to know past and future of that object and *yogi* gains *siddhi* which is kind of supernatural powers.

Power gained by *yogi*

- *Sanyama* on *purusha* - one obtains the power of knowledge, superphysical hearing, touching, seeing, tasting, and smelling, these (superphysical sense) are obstacles to *(nirbeeja) samadhi* but are *siddhis* (powers) are for worldly pursuits.
- loosening of bondages of *karma* - *yogi* get to know about the functioning of the *chitta* then he can enter into the body of another person.
- conquering vital force called *udana*- *yogi* does not sink in water, or in swamps, and he can walk on thorns.
- mastery on *samana* vital force - *yogi* can obtain divine radiance
- *sanyama* on the relation between *akasha* (Space)and ear- yogi can attain superphysical hearing ability.
- *sanyama* on relation of physical body, space and light matters like cotton- y*ogi* become very light and can fly.
- *samyama* on thought-waves of mind, when it is separated from body (*maha videha* or freedom from needs of body)–all coverings can be removed from the light of knowledge.
- *purusha* and *buddhi*- *yogi* attains power of omniscience and control over all states of existence.
- *sanyama* on the five gross and subtle elements on their nature, correlations and purpose- *yogi* have mastery over these gross elements and gains *siddhis* (power of becoming as tiny as an atom and all similar), then five gross elements and their characteristics cannot be barrier in the path of *yogi.*

Having control over the five gross elements, *yogi* attains the wealth of body like beauty, grace, strength and strong body. This accomplishment is called *kayasampat*

- By conquering senses- *yogi's* body becomes fast-moving like the mind, works through the senses without the body and acquires control over all organs created by *prakriti* (primordial matter).
- By establishing the distinction between *purusha* and *buddhi*- *yogi* attains power of omniscience and control over all states of existence.

Yogi gaining *siddhi*, which is power attained by *samyana* is called *Vibhuti*, but *yogi* should avoid enthusiasm or pride in the enticements of the celestial beings by this he is in danger of being caught once more by ignorance, and on receiving invitation from high places like from big clans or families or from big people, *yogi* should not be angry and proud, doing this again creates hindrances or distracting reasons in *yoga* practice, when a *yogi* is detached towards *siddhi* is called *vishoka* (power obtained after removing the veil of *Rajoguna* and *Tamoguna*) then all his troubles like ignorance etc. are destroyed, and *yogi* attains salvation.

Intellect and the *purusha* are totally different, intellect exist for the sake of *purusha*, while the *purusha* is for its own sake, by not understanding this difference is the cause of all experience, by *samyama* on the distinction, one gets knowledge of the *purusha* (pure consciousness).

Discriminative knowledge that simultaneously comprehends all objects in all conditions is the intuitive knowledge which brings liberation, and absolute freedom occurs when the lucidity of material nature and spirit are in pure equilibrium.

Kaivalya pada **(Independence)** - Many *siddhis* (Powers) arise in *yogi* by birth of *yogi*, or by taking medicines, chanting mantras, observing penance or by following *samadhi* (deep meditation) by this *yogi* gets a new and powerful body with changes that occurred in body, mind, mind and senses, good deeds, etc. are not the direct causes of changes in nature, but they act as breakers of obstacles to evolutions of nature, it is like a farmer breaking down barrier to let the water flow which then runs down by its own nature.

C*hitta* (minds stuff) are constructed from *asmita* (self-consciousness), and mind is director or mover of the many minds in many different activities, and salvation attained by *dhyana* (meditation) which is desireless, and *karma* of the *yogi* is neither *rajas* nor *tamas,* while *karma* of others is of three kinds *sattvik, rajas or tamas,* these three types of *karma* are in accordance to their deeds and person gets their fruits and enjoyments in the form of desires i.e. *sanskaras* (Latent impressions). Relation of cause and effect even though separated by locality and time, is because of memory and impressions (*samskara)* are same in form, and it is due to continuity and willingness to survive for those lustful latent impressions, and this cycle is going on from eternal time, where conservation of the lust which creates latent impressions (*samskara)* is done by cause, effect, support, and objects, hence in the absence of these four lust is also absent and so as the *samskara* is destroyed.

Forms and expression changes in accordance to time which are past, present or future and, since past and future both already exist within the object, hence it is matters which are present at all times and it manifest in form of subtle elements and are composed of the three *gunas* (qualities) of the things that are known or unknown to mind, however it is dependent on colouring which they give to mind, because *atman* which is lord of the mind, is unchangeable and fluctuations of mind are always known to *atman,* while *chitta* or mind-stuff is not self-luminous because it is an object of perception by the *purusha* or self and it is impossible for it to be of both ways (as perceiver and perceived) at the same time, If one postulates a second mind to perceive the first, then one would have to postulate an infinite number of minds and it would cause confusion of memory, where pure consciousness of the *atman* or self is unchangeable, and when reflection of its consciousness falls upon mind, then mind takes the form of the *atman* or self and appears to be conscious, and mind is able to perceive because it reflects both *atman* or self and the objects of perception.

Mind-stuff or *chitta* exists for the sake of *purusha* or consciousness, because it can act only in association with It, though it is having countless desires but by knowledge of discrimination, it eliminates all curiosities that arise in *yogi* about himself and when mind is focused on the practice of discrimination, and it moves toward liberation. Distractions due to past impressions or *samskara* may arise if mind relaxes its discrimination, even for a moment, while it has impression of the past life, that too can be finished by same process as the removal of afflictions due to *karma*. In case one can maintain constant state of *vairagya* or dispassion even in most exalted state of enlightenment and does not get attracted towards the *siddhis*(superpowers) then it attains "*dharma megha samadhi*" which is end of sufferings, ignorance and *karmic* collections.

By removal of all afflictions as result of *karmas*, which is due to covering of ignorance is eliminated by itself through *vairagya* or dispassion and *yogi* gets knowledge of purest form which is known to very few, and *gunas* or qualities terminate their sequence of transformations because they have fulfilled their purpose, sequence referred here is an uninterrupted succession of moments which can be recognized at the end of their transformations and since *gunas* no longer have any purpose to serve for *atman* or self and they revert to *prakriti* or nature, this process is called liberation, where *atman* shines forth in its own pristine nature, as pure consciousness.

NYAYA PHILOSOPHY

Nyaya which literally means justice, equality for all being, especially in context to collection of general or universal rules, it is the theory of logic, and the term also refers to an argument consisting of an enthymeme (argument where conclusion is not explicit for example " A bird has feathers, therefore, it flies. (Animals with feathers fly)" or sometimes with syllogism (two separate statements used to prove third statement example "All mangoes are fruits, some fruits are sweet, therefore some mangoes are sweet" In philosophical context.

This philosophy is based on valid reasoning to acquire knowledge of reality, according to the *Nyaya* philosophy, human suffering results from mistakes/defects produced by activity under wrong knowledge (notions and ignorance) and *Moksha* (liberation) is gained through right knowledge, one needs to have reliable means to gain correct knowledge and to remove wrong notions. False knowledge is not merely ignorance but also includes delusion whereas correct knowledge is discovering and overcoming one's delusions, and understanding true nature of soul, self and reality, Knowledge manifests with *Padarthas* or elements is "categories of logic" and by understanding their source, truth will become illumined while this philosophy make use of *pramanas* (source or instruments of knowledge) for the purpose of gaining correct knowledge, by which we perceive objects itself is a *Pramana* or means of knowledge.

Sixteen *padarthas* or elements are required to ascertain truth, out of which first nine are based to logic to be followed and later seven are for preventing and mitigating errors in knowledge, if we have knowledge of *padarthas* or elements and by developing detachment that will lead to liberation, it is a state in which we know neither sorrow nor happiness.

1. *Pramanas* or means of knowledge accepted are of four kinds

- Direct perception or *pratyaksha*, It is knowledge that arises due to the association of self, mind, sense organs with objects, it is of two kinds ordinary (direct experience of reality by eyes, ears, nose, touch and taste) and extraordinary (induction from perceived specifics to a universal like intuition, telepathy etc), it denotes two stages of perception, *nirvikalpa* (indeterminate), where it perceives an object without being able to know its features, and the second *savikalpa* (determinate), when one is able to clearly know an object, all *laukika* (ordinary) and *alaukika* (extra ordinary) are *savikalpa*, if an object is perceived with its name we have determinate perception but if it is perceived without a name, we have indeterminate perception which is an apprehends substance, by its qualities and actions and it's perception will be universals, but a separate and indistinct without any association with any names.

- Inference or *Anumana*, it is of two types, inference for oneself or *Svarthanumana*, where one does not need any formal procedure, and at the most the last three of their five steps, and inference for others or *Parathanumana*, which requires a systematic methodology of five steps.

Steps of *anumana* (inference)

1. There is fire on the hill (called *Pratijna*, required to be proved)
2. Because there is smoke on hill (called *Hetu*, reason)
3. Wherever there is smoke, there is fire, (called *Udaharana*, example of *vyapti*)
4. The hill has smoke that is pervaded by fire (called *Upanaya*, reaffirmation or application)
5. Therefore, there is fire on the hill (called *Nigamana*, conclusion)

Inference is false when, unproved, irregular and contradictory *hetu* (reason) is used for reasoning

Inference can also be classified into three types, *Purvavat* which is inferring an unperceived effect from a perceived cause like perceiving rain from dark cloud, *Sheshavat* which is inferring an unperceived cause from a perceived effect like perceiving rain from swollen river and *Samanyatodrishta* when inference is not based on causation but on uniformity of co-existence like if we see smoke in a distant location, there is likely a fire there as well , *anumana* or inference could be false is not applied appropriately.

- Comparison or *Upamana* means comparison and analogy, knowledge arises out of the relation between a name and the object it denotes is regarded as comparison. Subject of comparison is called *upameyam*, object of comparison is alled *upamanam*, while the attribute(s) are identified as *samanya*.

> **Example of *Upamana* (comparison)**
>
> If a traveller who has never visited land with wildlife is told, by someone who has been there, that in those lands you will see an animal that looks like kind of cow, grazes like cow but is different from a cow. It helps the traveller identify the new animal later

- *Sabda* or testimony is a valid source of knowledge, testimony of past or present by reliable and trustworthy person, it is accepted that human being needs to know numerous facts, and with the limited time and energy available, he can learn only a fraction of those facts and truths directly, he must rely on others, his parent, family, friends, teachers, ancestors and kindred members of society to rapidly acquire and share knowledge and thereby enrich each other's lives.

2. *Prameya* or object of true knowledge, it has twelve objects of knowledge to be known

   - *Sarira* or body, which includes body and mind, it has ten senses which reacts to the external stimuli. *Atman* (self) is an experiencer of result of actions strives to attain pleasure and avoid displeasure

- *Atman* (self), six factors indicate presence of self as an experiencer
    - *Jana* – knowledge of things
    - *Prayatna* – striving
    - *Raga* – attachment
    - *Dvesha* – aversion
    - *Sukha* – pleasure
    - *Dukha* – pain
- *Indriyas* (senses) and *Artha* (experience), there are seven field of senses which demonstrate existence of being as five elements (*punchbhutas*), which are revealed with five senses and have five experiences of being.

Indriyas (senses)	→	**Bhutas (Elements)**	→	**Artha (experience / Object it revels)**
• *Ghrana* (smell)		• *Prathivi* (Earth)		• *Gandha* (Odor)
• *Rasna* (Taste)		• *Apas*(water)		• *Rasa* (Flavor)
• *Cakshu* (Vision)		• *Tejas* (Fire)		• *Rupa* (Color)
• *Tvak* (Touch)		• *Vayu* (Air)		• *Sparsha* (Sensation)
• *Srotra* (Hearing)		• *Akasha* (Ether/ space)b		• *Sabda* (Sound)

Senses and their objects provide five varieties of perception yielding special kinds of knowledge according to the objects which they reveal.

- *Buddhi* or intelligence is a mental power which enables one to reflect upon the teachings and to contemplate self
- *Manas* or mind is an intellect (*buddhi*), which seeks factual knowledge, that is external and worldly, while the mind

(*manas*) aims at internal knowledge that is wisdom which is spiritual

Seven field of senses

1. *Dravya* (substance) – Nine substance as material cause of things are *Privathi* (earth), *Ap* (water), *Tejas* (light), *Vayu* (air), *Dig* (dimensions), *Akasha* (space), *Kala* (time), *Atman* (self) and *Manas* (mind)
2. *Guna* (qualities)- Attributes to *Dravya,* these are twenty-four in number which are – colour, taste, odour, touch, number, dimension, separateness, conjunction & disjunction, nearness & remoteness (both space and time), heaviness, fluidity, viscosity (smoothness of water), sound, knowledge, pleasure (gratification), suffering, desire (attachment), aversion, effort, merit & demerit and faculty (velocity, impression and elasticity)
3. *Kriya* (action) – upwards, downwards, horizontal movement, circular, contracting and contracting
4. *Samanvya* (Generality) – all the known objects although different from one another are still substance (*dravya*). Their being substance is the higher generalization. But these objects can be further divided into different classes, each class differing from the others but having an individual or lower generality, like certain group of animals are called cow etc.
5. *Visesa* (Individuality) - all matter is composed of atoms and each atom is a unit, therefore there are an infinite number of individual units.
6. *Samavaya* (Inherence) - intimate relationship that exists between a substance and its attributes or qualities, between atoms and their compounds, between the whole and its parts, between substance and its modifications.
7. *Abhava* (nonexistence) – like cold in fire

- *Pravrtti* or extrovert activity, it sets the mind, body, and voice in motion, for good or bad, it is stimulated by craving (*tṛṣṇa*) arising from false knowledge (*avidya*) that leads to bondage (*bandhana*) and eventually to suffering and transmigration (*saṃsara*)

- *Dosha* or distorted view, it is initiating causes of all actions, attraction (*raga*) and aversion (*dwesa*) are two polarities which in combination create delusion

*Dhosa (*Distorted view)	Manifestation
Raga (attraction)	Leads to attachment in form of lust, greed, craving, selfishness, longing, and covetousness
Dwesa (aversion)	Leads to forbearance in form of anger, envy, jealousy, and implacability
*Abhinivesa (*Delusion)	Leads to misapprehension in form of clinging, grasping, attachment, immersion

- *Phala* or consequences, where every activity (*kriya*) has an outcome which is either pleasure (*sukha*) or pain (*duḥkha*) to ourself or to others, depending upon the nature of the action done, *phala* can be immediate or with the time lapse, it is seen that fruit of right conduct or *karma-phala* done in previous lives, manifest currently in this world, it may appear as together (*sahatva*), progeny (*praja*) and wealth (*vittam*), which are sources of worldly joy.
- *Dukha* or suffering, it an impediment to self-realization, default human condition is dissatisfaction because everything is impermanent, unstable and unsubstantial. It can be said that one who is addicted to pleasure, in reality is in pain but when there is no pleasure in attainment and enjoyment, pain in some form or other is not present.
- *Pratyabhava* or rebirth, birth is connection of the *jivatman* (soul) with a new body and mind, where birth is not a production of a new circumstance, but only a re-association, while death is not the destruction of anything, but only separation, to deny this principle would be to negate law of universe.

- *Apavarga* or liberation, it is an absolute freedom from suffering, only *atman* (self) is liberated from the body, sense-organs and intellect is freed from *duḥkha* or pain. When mind is awakened to true nature of things by means of the cultivation of right Knowledge, *duḥkha* fade away as the darkness of the night before the rising sun. Distorted views (*doṣas*) will dissipate, and there will be no incentive for motivated actions which are action done with a desire for rewards, in turn it will free self from future rebirths.

3. *Samasya* or doubt, it is conflicting judgment about the precise character of an object, due to

    - properties common to many objects, like rope appears to be snake
    - properties not common to any of the objects, like accepting kangaroo as big rat
    - conflicting testimony by two or more people
    - irregularity of perception and non-perception, like delusion of pond and mirage doubts are desirable, since it is due to incomplete knowledge and there is incentive for further investigation to arrive at true knowledge, however error in understanding is not desirable since it creates erroneous convections and sedate mind and gets no incentive in further investigation of truth.

4. *Prayojana* or motive, it is desire which impels to act, purpose is motive behind all action, it may be to attain something pleasurable or to avoid something undesirable, unless there is purpose there can be no successful action, and a wise person never engages in purposeless action.

5. *Drstanta* or Illustration or corroborative instances, it is where layman and an expert entertain the same opinion, like when there is rain there must have clouds.

6. *Siddhanta* or established theory), it is a conclusion that is recognised as being logically proven by a certain school of philosophy and are of four types

- commonly accepted truth — not opposed by any school of philosophy and which is claimed by at least one school, example all schools of *hindu* philosophy accept earth, water, light, air, and ether as the basic five elements, and smell, taste, colour, touch, and sound as the objects of the five senses.
- peculiar truth — accepted by similar schools, but rejected by opposite schools, example abrahamic schools all accept that God creates the world from nothing, whereas all schools of Indian philosophy reject this conclusion, as a something cannot come into existence out of nothing
- consequential truth —if one is accepted, leads to the acceptance of another example, acceptance of the doctrine that self is separate from the five senses, implies that senses are more than one and each of the senses has its particular object and self-derives its knowledge through the channels of the senses and substance which is distinct from its qualities is the locus of them.
- implied truth —not explicitly declared as such, but which follows from the examination of particulars concerning it example, discussion whether certain people should be allowed to vote implies that those people are capable of understanding and making political decisions

7. *Avayava* or factors of reasoning, where inference (*anumana*) is the process of knowing something, not by means of contact between the senses and physical objects or not by observation, but rather through the medium of a sign which is invariably related to it, hence inference involves the process of analysing,

memories, correlations, propositions, theories and arguments, it has two applications

- *svartha* - reasoning for oneself to gain correct knowledge by reflective thinking about something to convince oneself of a truth, or to discard a misconception.
- *parartha* - reasoning to convince another for correct knowledge.

8. *Hetvabhasa* or fallacious reasoning, where reasoning is erroneous if logic in any part of syllogism is applied inappropriately, example
   - The Irregular middle or the ambiguous - "All beings that live in Himalayas are saints, tigers live in the Himalayas and therefore tigers are saints", is erroneous since tigers and saints as well as many other beings live in Himalayas and conclusion of this inference cannot be said to be correct, because the middle term, Himalayan beings, is not always related to the major term saints.
   - Self-contradictory – "Sound is eternal because it is produced, everything produced is impermanent", reason contradicts to one to be proved, because eternal is never produced.
   - Inconclusive – "body is non-eternal, because it does not possess the attribute of eternality", reason is asking question, for "noneternal" is the same as "not possessing the attribute of eternality."
   - Non-sequitur – " All *Hindus* are vegetarians because they all believe in *ahimsa*", conclusion does not logically follow from the previous argument or statement.
   - Contradicted – "Fire is cool"
9. *Tarka* or hypothetical reasoning, it is a method of arriving at truth by negating all competing ideas, example "Self a product

or a non-Product", This is not a method which ascertains, determines or verifies that self is a particular thing or not, but it eliminates all other contesting theories which supports, after which truth is established through the application of other means of right knowledge, it is a supporting technique and is, therefore mentioned separately.

10. *nirṇaya* or dialectic, in this form of dialogue between two people who may hold differing views yet wish to establish the truth by seeking agreement with one another.

11. *Vada* or discussion, it is dialogue in which one adopts one of two opposing positions, in contrast to *nirnaya* two or more people hold differing views and wish to persuade or prove one another wrong (and thus a jury or judge is needed to decide the matter).

12. *Jalpa* or polemic, it is kind of wrangle, where it consists of mere attacks on the opposite side and only interest is to heckle speaker by carping and offering frivolous objections. It may be used as means of protecting fragile knowledge which has not yet matured or If one's philosophy or belief is under attack then one may employ this negative means for self-defence.

13. *vitaṇḍa* or cavil, it is mere attacks on the opposite side, where one may occasionally encounter objectionable people who, devoid of true knowledge, are puffed up with their academic achievements or are deluded by their own erroneous convictions, and these people may try to impose their views and beliefs on others.

14. *Chala* or casuistry, it is by use of clever but unsound reasoning and can be of three kind

    - *Vacas* or playing with words - wilfully taking a term to mean something different from that intended by the speaker, example 'quadruped' to mean four-legged table instead of an animal.

- *Samanyas* or generalization - asserting the impossibility of a particular part because of the impossibility of the entirely example to deny that a particular cow is black because all cows are not black.
- *Upacaras* or metaphor - invalidating a word used in a particular context by taking it literally when it was used metaphorically, example 'House cheered' means that the people in the house cheered and not the physical house.

15. *Jaati* or futile rejoinder - reply is said to be futile if it does not take into consideration the universal connection between the middle term and the major term in syllogism, just a similarity or dissimilarity is not sufficient to establish, example If someone asks , "are you painting" when you are holding paint can and a brush, your rejoinder could be, "No, I'm just doing my nails."
16. *nigraha-sthana* or clinchers- if one misunderstands their own statement or the other's statement, then they are considered defeated, this can happen when one's questions whether a statement is relevant, and it is of no purpose in enter into a debate with one who demonstrates lack of understanding of the subject being investigated, one is advised to stop discussion moment other demonstrates an ignorance , or misunderstanding of the subject under discussion.

Theory of causation in *Nyaya* philosophy upholds *astkaryavada* which states that effect is not same as the cause and effect is a new creation or a new bringing of its existence, effect did not exist in the material cause prior to its production, whereas for liberation it believes that bondage of the world is due to false knowledge, which can be removed by constantly thinking of its opposite called *pratipakshabhavana* and the true knowledge is gained, however it also mentions that God's grace is essential for obtaining true knowledge.

There is innumerable self that exists in the universe and self-possesses consciousness, where self is trapped by the law of *karma* hence, suffering and pain are the obvious phenomenon, to get rid from all sorts of sufferings the self seeks liberation. God is the creator, sustainer and destroyer of the universe, and he regulates earth, solar systems and the movements of planets and becomes identified as an omnipresent and omniscience being in the cosmos and world is created out of the four eternal atoms as its material cause, these are, space, time, mind and soul, while God being efficient cause of universe is responsible for its maintenance, and destruction thus God, is the first efficient cause of the universal forces so he is the creator of the world. God is one, infinite, eternal, and the universe with space and time or mind and soul does not limit him, and God is said to possess six perfections, which are infinite glory, absolute sovereignty, unqualified virtue, supreme beauty, perfect knowledge, and complete detachment.

Nyaya philosophy offers an argument to establish the existence of God known as causal argument, on this line of argument, it is stated that the entire universe is constituted of enumerable elements both subtle and gross and a human being by possessing limited knowledge cannot be the creator of universe, this implies the creator is one who is beyond space and time and must be eternal and devoid of all limitations, and all these features are therein supreme being or God, hence God is the creator or designer of the universe, hence according to the *nyaya* philosophy, God is the creator, sustainer and destroyer of the universe and he is the efficient cause or having skill of creation, but not the material cause of the universe, material cause of this universe is the eternal atoms which are earth, water, fire, and air and God desires that universe to remains in the state of stability and tranquillity by having real knowledge of all objects and its occurrences, hence he is omnipresent and omniscient being.

Nyaya philosophy says that there are infinite number of individual self or soul that exists in the universe and all soul have perceivable qualities like pleasure, pain, etc. but they are eternal and all-pervading and, that self can neither be identified with mind or *manas* nor can be identified with pure consciousness but it can be understood as consciousness belonging to an individual, because mind is atomic and unperceivable and hence devoid from perceivable qualities. On the other hand, consciousness belongs to the individual self or soul but not same as self, hence consciousness is not the self or soul but only an attribute of the self or soul, which is an accidental attribute of the self. Self or soul in its original state has no consciousness and hence devoid of cognition and knowledge, but when it comes to contact with sense organs it acquires consciousness.

Self or soul is regarded *ahamkara* or I-consciousness, as the knower and it is known through internal perception only, since there is self consequently there is bondage and hence, soul aspires for liberation or salvation, where liberation is the state devoid of all kinds of sufferings and bondage caused due to self or soul's association with body and sense organs and as long as self or soul is attached with body and sense organs, it goes through the cycles of birth and death, which is law of *karma*, while liberation can be achieved when there is cessation of *karmic* chain or *karmic* influx and is a state where self is detached from body and sense organs.

VAISHESHIKA PHILOSOPHY

Name *Vaiseṣika* derives from *viseṣa,* which is category that represents individuality of innumerable existing objects, although *vaiseṣika* system developed independently from the *nyaya* philosophy, but two became similar and are often studied together. However, in its classical form, the *vaiseṣika* school differed from *nyaya* in a significant way, *nyaya* accepted four (direct observation, inference, comparison and testimony) sources of valid knowledge and *vaiseṣika* accepted two (direct observation and inference) with *vedas* being reliable and valid mean of knowledge.

Vaisesika is a dualistic philosophy with soul and material objects being two different existences, where God has created all out from nothing and creation and dissolution happens at his wish, God imparts motion to motionless atoms and is the cause of creation of world, God is authority of *vedas* and is the principal cause of *karma.*

Vaiseṣika school is known for its insights in naturalism, a form of atom in natural philosophy that all reality is composed of five substances (earth, water, air, fire, and space), each of these five are of two types, *paramaṇu* (atom) and its composite, It postulated that all objects in the physical universe are reducible to *paramaṇu* (atoms), and one's experiences are derived from the interplay of *drvya* or substance which is function of atoms and their number and their spatial arrangements, its *guna* (quality), *karma* (activity), *samanya* (commonness), (*vishesha)* particularity and *samavaya* (inherence).

Whatever human beings perceive is composite, and even the smallest perceptible thing, like fleck of dust, has parts, which are therefore invisible, smallest composite thing as a triad or *tryaṇuka* with three parts, each part with a dyad or *dyaṇuka* and a dyad further has two parts, each of which is an atom, size, form, truths and everything that human beings experience as a whole is a function of *parmanus* or atom according to their number and their spatial arrangements, but the aggregation and nature of these atoms was predetermined by cosmic forces.

Bondage of soul to the material object is due to ignorance of soul and liberation is attained by knowledge and complete understanding of the world of experience, soul is the performer of action which is eighter confirmatory to *veda* as good action and non-confirmatory to *veda* as bad action, good and bad actions are due to *karmic* influx and law of *karma* guided by God, bondage continues to remain till soul performs action.

Liberation of soul is by realization of its true nature, which is distinct of body and mind and is not affected by desires and passion, liberation is with all associated *gunas* (qualities) as suffering, pain, desire and pleasure, soul devoid of substance and qualities are devoid of consciousness also hence this state is unwarranted.

In *vaisheshika,* and its metaphysics or *tatwa mimansa* is essence of reality, variety, diversity and plurality, and seven objects or *padarthas* are said as knowable or *Jneya* and nameable or *Abhidhaya* , and these are to be known by the means of two proof or *pramanas,* which are perception and inference are the means required to ascertain truth, unlike *nyaya* philosophy where sixteen *padarthas* are needed by four *pramanas.* One with the knowledge of *padarthas* or objects and by developing detachment to it will lead to liberation, it is a state in which we know neither sorrow nor happiness.

1. *Dravya* or substance are real and have objective existence which differs from each other by unique qualities and actions it performs, however qualities and actions can be separated from substance or *Dravya,* but substance itself is inherent cause of the effect, there are two kinds of *Dravya* or substance

a. Eternal -which cannot be further divided.

- Time *(kala)*
- Space / ether *(Dik)*
- Self *(Atman)*
- Mind *(manas)*

b. Non eternal – *Panch bhutas* or five elements, which can be further divided to smaller parts and their associated *gunas* (qualities) are

- Earth (*Prithivi*) having *guna* (quality) of smell.
- Water (*Jal*) having *guna* (quality) of taste
- Fire (*Tej*) having *guna* (quality) of colour
- Air (*Vayu*) having *guna* (quality) of touch
- Ether (*Akasha*) having *guna* (quality) of sound

These *guna* (qualities) are perceived by five sensory organs which are nose, tongue, eye, skin and ears respectively.

Different *gunas* (qualities) of substance		
Colour	Conjugation	Aversion
Taste	Dis- Junction	Effort
Smell	Nearness	Heaviness
Touch	Remoteness	Fluidity
Sound	Cognition	Viscidity
Number	Pleasure	Tendency
Magnitude	Pain	Moral merit
Distinctiveness	Desire	Moral demerit

2. *Guna* or qualities is subset of substance, it is of passive in nature and do not produce any object and one quality do not overlap with other quality or are mutually exclusive, while action or *kriya* is performed by substance not by its quality, It is not inherent to substance but is acquired by substance, there are twenty-four different *gunas* or qualities which are present in substance.

3. Action or *karma* is dynamic unlike *guna* which is static and like *guna, karma* also reside in substance. Karma is perceived and inferred by mind, and are classified as five types

   a. Upward motion

   b. Downward motion

   c. Contraction

   d. Expansion

   e. Locomotion

4. Generality or *Samanya* is for individual members of the group having some common qualities are grouped together by virtue of its common qualities and are referred by common name, it is of three types based on common quality or common action

   a. *Para- Samanya* or most comprehensive, it signifies the most extensive or superior generality, encompassing a wider range of objects, which applies to all substances, attributes, and actions example animal as it encompasses all animals

   b. *Apara- Samanya* or less comprehensive, representing a narrower scope of beinghood, such as cow among the animals or *dravyatva* or substance-hood, *gunatva* or quality-hood, and *karmatva* or action-hood.

   c. *Parapara- Samanya* or belongingness, it is level of generality that lies between the most comprehensive (*para*) and the least comprehensive (*apara*), example "beinghood" or *satta*, which is more general than "men" (*apara*) but less general than "animal" (*para*) and it covers all living beings, including animals, but also things that are not animals, like plants.

Generality is not a quality of action of similar objects, but it is a name only, otherwise it has no existence, and it is not something from outside entering to individual but is universal and particular details are same as apprehended by mind or intellect.

5. Particularity or *Vaisesa*, it is opposite to generality which is unique and specific to the individual of eternal substance (atoms, space, time, and the self), enabling us to perceive them as distinct from one another. It is crucial as it allows us to perceive and understand the individuality of substances.
6. Inherence or *Samavaya* is a fundamental concept, category, representing an inseparable and having eternal relationship between two entities that cannot exist independently, it binds together different entities and is crucial for understanding the structure of the universe, their inseparable relationship between two things that are not perceptible but inferred from their inseparable connection, for example
    a. Part and Whole (*Avayava-Avayavi)* which is relationship, between part and the whole of which it is a part of like relation of yarn and cloth, clay and pot
    b. Generic and Individual (*Jaati*-Vyakti) relationship between a general category and a specific instance like red cow among the cows
    c. Quality and Substance (*Guṇa - Dravya*) relationship between a quality and the substance that possesses it like fire has heat
    d. Cause and Effect (*Karaṇa- Karyya*) relationship between cause and its effect

7. Nonexistence or *Abhava* is the absence of certain quality or action and are of two types
    - *Sansargabhava* or absence of one entity in another, example, coolness in fire, squareness in circle, etc. it again are of three kinds
        - *Paragbhava* or antecedent is non existing like pot is not existent in clay prior to its making, hence when antecedent is non existing then it has no beginning or end
        - *Dhvansabhava* or subsequently not existing is not existing after destruction of it like absence of pot when destroyed
        - *Atyantabhava* or absolute non-existent is absence of one thing in another all the time in past, present or future like coolness in fire
    - *Anyonyabhava or* mutual nonexistence is if one thing exists other do not exist like if table exist then horse do not exist in table hence for eternal things which are different from each other are excluded from one another all the time

Relation of quality or *guna* and substance or *Dravya* exist in substance not depending on the one's perception while effect does not exist in cause and effect is not identical to cause also, hence each of the effect is the new beginning. All material objects are composed of minute parts called atom or *anu*, and all objects are subject of creation and destruction, atoms are said to be of four kinds which are earth, water, air and fire and its combination in various proportions along with its qualities of each are responsible for creation.

God is the authority of the *Veda* and believes in the principal law of *karma*, *Veda* is authoritative because it is the word of God, which is supreme soul, perfect, omniscient, omnipresent and eternal and is the guiding principle controlling the motion of atoms, he is guided by the law of *karma* representing the unseen power of merits and demerits, he creates motion that the living beings may be rewarded and punished according to their past deeds. God creates universe out of nothing, he is the creator in the sense that he is the designer and architect of the universe, creation and destruction of the universe takes place at his wish, in this perspective *vaisesika* atom is spiritual and God as the creator imparts motion to atoms which originally lack motion and creation does not start until God sets the atoms in motion, hence God is the efficient cause of the world not the material cause.

Human beings are in bondage because of their ignorance, and they can be liberated from bondage by knowing and applying knowledge that, action by the soul which causes bondage and liberation, if actions are in conformity to *Vedic* injunctions, then they are considered as good, and if they are prohibited by the *Veda's* injunction, then they are bad, good and bad actions result to soul as its *karmic* influx, it states that every action has its own fruits or results, hence good actions results in good fruits and bad actions results in bad fruits, whereas liberation is the cessation of all sufferings, passions, inclinations, desires, along with pain, pleasures, and all qualities, it is pure, quality less, indeterminate, where liberated soul exists as a substance devoid of all qualities and no consciousness, hence the liberated soul is unwarranted. Law of *karma* being the prime cause of bondage is guided by God, he imparts motion to the atoms and leads to creation for the sake of pleasure and pain of the individual soul, as long as soul performs action, bondage remains and once soul realizes its true nature as distinct from the mind and body, it is no longer is affected by desire and passion and liberation is achieved.

PURVA MIMANSA

First major orthodox philosophical system develop was *Purva Mimamsa*, this orthodox system accepts authority of the *Vedas* only.

Sanskrit word *mimamsa* means a revered thought and word is originated from the root where man which refers to thinking or investigating, word *mimamsa* also suggests probing and acquiring knowledge or critical review and investigation of the *Vedas.*

Each of the *Vedas* is composed of four parts, *Samhitas, Brahmanas, Aranyakas* and *Upanishads,* first two parts are generally focused on rituals, and they form the *Karma-kanda* portion of the *Vedas* and later two parts forms *Jyana-kanda* (concerned with knowledge) portion of the *Vedas.*

Purva-Mimamsa is based on the earlier (*Purva* or earlier) parts of the *Vedas* and *Uttar Mimamsa* is based on the later (*Uttar* or later) parts of the *Vedas.*

Purva-Mimamsa is also known as *Karma Mimamsa* since it deals with the *Karmic* actions of rituals and sacrifices. *Uttar-Mimamsa* is also known as *Brahman Mimamsa* since it is concerned with the knowledge of reality, former deals with *dharma* and the latter with *brahman* in popular terms, *Purva-Mimamsa* is known simply as *Mimamsa* and *Uttar-Mimamsa* as *Vedanta.*

Earlier scholars wrote commentaries on *Mimamsa-Sutra* (aphorism) and they were lost with the passage of time however earliest available commentary is *Sabara-bhasya,* which is an authoritative basis of all subsequent works on *Mimamsa, Kumarila Bhatta* and *Prabhakara* independently wrote their commentaries on *Sabara-bhasya,* while *Mandan Mishra,* was a follower of *Kumarila Bhatta* also wrote a commentary, but at a later stage he changed his thinking and became a disciple of *Shankaracharya* of *vedantic* philosophy.

Mimansa accepts *Vedas* as the eternal source by which truth is revealed, it differs from the earlier four philosophical systems (*Vaisheshika, Nyaya, Samkhya, Yoga* which neither accept nor reject the authority of the *Vedas* on performance of rituals.

Mimamsa system gives importance to verbal testimony, which is essentially the *Vedic* testimony, it accepts 'Word" or the '*Shabda*' as the only means of knowledge and strongly contends that the *Vedas* are not authored by an individual but are 'self-revealed' or '*apaurusheya*' and they manifest their own validity.

This philosophy is a pluralistic and realist, it endorses that reality of world as well as that of individual souls is that, soul is accepted as an eternal and infinite substance, while consciousness is an accidental attribute of the soul and soul is distinct from body, senses and mind, earlier *Mimamsa* scholars do not give much importance to the deities, and they do not endorse God as the creator of the universe.

This system has a profound faith in *Vedas* and supports the law of *karma*, it believes in unseen power or *apurva*, and also accepting heaven and hell and supports theory of liberation. *Purva mimansa* by sage *Jaimini* has twelve chapters in six sections, it defines rules for interpretation of *vedas* and it presents material activity and its result as entire reality, stating that cycle of *karma* is perpetual and aim for performing activity is to have birth in higher stratum among *devas or* Gods and, primary purpose of *vedas* is to engage humans in rituals for creating good *karmas, mimansa* emphasises on *dharma* or duty as prescribed in *vedas* over the knowledge and states that by performing *dharma* or righteous duty as per *veda* will create good *karma* and that enables one to have birth among higher beings as *devas* or God.

If desire arises to know righteous duties or *dharma*, then one must learn text and meanings of injunctions in *vedas*, since dharma has no definition as it cannot be defined by the worldly knowledge and *dharma* or righteous duty is beyond this world, hence *dharma* is not amenable by sense of perception as it is not an object existing at the time of perception but are brought into existence by performance of correct actions. Authority of *vedas* is the only mean recognised for knowledge of *dharma* or righteous duty, whose validity is beyond all disputes and relation of words with its meaning in *vedas* is unborn and eternal, since injunctions as part of *vedas* are also eternal and, are the only valid means of knowing *dharma*, word is said to be eternal since effort to pronounce does not creates the word but it is in existence prior to effort, while word is manifested by an agency for momentary perception only and modification to word can be done, which is possible only for the things already in existence, word uttered by one is understood same by all in past, present or future and it was same in time immortal, further no cause or agent for destruction of word is perceptible like other objects hence once produced then words are indestructible. Word and its associated meaning are eternal hence sentence formed by combination of words are also eternal, further *vedas* are not the work of one author however certain sections of *vedas* is named after individuals, which are not written by them but certain sections of special studies are done by some person of that name who is regarded as specialist in that section of *veda* or it may be just by chance that name resembles to certain sound of name.

Authority of *arthavada* which is statements or declarations that encourage or discourage certain actions by emphasizing the good or bad consequences of performing or omitting them, often through praise, censure, or examples, with the words connected synthetically to *vedic* injunctions are for reason of praising the word which is enjoined to it, however incongruity will not apply to such modifications since words in passage are not to be taken in literal sense, whereas *vedic* injunctions have indirect application also, where it have contradictions, hence are justified when injunctions are modified for *arthavada*, it is sometimes used to praise knowledge and its universality which pertains to capability to perform all actions which leads to result due to action, however results in every cases may differ due to magnitude of action and sometime results are impossible to negate.

Vedic Injunctions must tell something new otherwise its description is useless when used in ordinary parlance, facts told in such passage is to be taken along with other *vedic* injunctions for the case compatible with context and removal of it will make *vedic* injunctions useless, case where *vedic* injunctions appears to contain certain course of action then it does not require any support to the statement of reason of the action, since *vedas* are self-sufficient in authority.

Use of *vedic mantras* or phrase must be regarded as intended and significant for the occasion, it has useful bearing on *dharma* or duty and purpose is not the recitation alone, in some cases *vedic mantras* are found not conveying any information and are useful for the performance of sacrifice or *yagya*, in that case it may be taken for recitation only, which has transcendental results.

Greatest authority of *vedas* is knowing *dharma* or duty is *vedic* declarations or injunctions, if in contradictions with *smriti* or by someone memory or someone experience, then authority of *vedas* is to be adopted, if *smriti* does not contradict with *vedas* text, then that can be taken in support of *smritis* to *vedas*, otherwise there is no authority to *smriti*, in the case where *smriti* has its origin from worldly object, but no such worldly motive is found in it then it is considered useful.

Word should be taken in sense attributed in scripture and knowledge of *dharma* is to be acquired by *vedic* scripture alone, in case equivalent word is not available or meaning of word cannot be absolutely ascertained in other language then meaning is to be looked in etymology in the context it is used, examples of some of the texts and their usage in knowledge of *dharma*

- *Kalpasutra*, manual of religious practice emerged from various schools of *vedas*, it explains procedures for performing rituals which are sacrificial rituals *(Shruta sutra)* which are domestic rituals (*Grihya sutra*) and conduct in life (*Dharma sutra*), as this manual though defines *dharma* or duty but are of human origin hence is treated as *smritis or* by one's experience
- *Holakadhikarna*, is authority of popular customs however it is assumed that *vedic* text support local customs, but it cannot be qualified as specification since it is specific to the places etc, where text related to knowing *dharma* needs to be of universal authority
- *Vyakaran andhiparna*, is the grammar which is necessary for using correct form of the word, but is not a source of knowing *dharma*

Word and things denoted in *vedas* are of ordinary parlance and it is for the entire community not for individual or some group of people.

One action cannot be regarded as entirely different from another unless it has different transcendental results or *apurvas*, further distinction of actions is on primary and subsidiary action, primary leads to independent *apurvas*, while those actions that tends to merely complete primary action are subsidiary actions and have no distinct *apurvas* of their own. There is a different action related to different words and frequent repetition of word are taken as explanation to the context it is used, *sutras* or aphorism proceed to point of difference among actions are based on number, name and properties and difference in treatment of properties till commencement of treatment in different context.

Objection on difference of action based on difference of name, repetition, properties and context are elaborated in section of *mimansa*, such ascertainment of difference is necessary in knowing relationship of subservicing between actions, eligibility of person performing certain actions is only when *vedic* injunctions clearly comprehend that there can be a transference of properties of one action to another.

Mimamsa acknowledges the existence of deities mentioned in *Vedic* rituals but does not assign them a significant supreme status or focus on them as a creator or God, it focuses on the principle of *karma*, where actions have consequences and results are determined by the nature of actions performed, rather than divine intervention or the will of a higher power.

Mimamsa insists on eternal universe and self, which is distinct from the body and mind, it believes in existence of many individual souls where goal is liberation (*moksha*) from the cycle of rebirth which can be achieved through the exhaustion of *karma* not by the grace of God. *Mimamsa* is not an atheistic philosophy, but it accepts existence of soul, rebirth, *karma*, and *dharma*, but primary focus is on efficiency of *Vedic* rituals as *dharma* (duty) and principle of *karma*.

VEDANTA/ PRASTANTRI

prasthantri- principal *upnishads, Gita* and *Bhramsutra*

Commentary or *bhashyam* by *Adi Shankaracharyya*

Vedanta literally means "end of *vedas*" and are considered foundation of *advita* or non-duality philosophy, three primary text which constituent of *vedantic* philosophy are termed as "*prasthantri*" means exit with trio are *upnishad, bhagwatgita* and *brahmsutra.*

All these are considered valid means of knowledge since all of it derived based on, *Shruti* – knowledge transferred verbally over generations from time primordial, are considered most reliable, *Smriti* – based on experience of revered person and *Yukti* – based on reasoning, each of the *prasthantri* text are based on one of these themes.

- *Upnashid – Shruti prasthan* (Revelation), there are 108 *upnishads* and ten are considered principle *upnishads* for the purpose of *vedantic* studies
- *Bhagwatgita or Gita – Smriti prasthana (Anubhava* – experience), oral testimony by lord himself
- *Bhramsutra – Naya prasthana (Yukti* – reasoning), establishing *vedantic* philosophy by refutation of other competing philosophy and synchronizing all *upnishads* written at different timelines by different sects but having basis on *vedas,* it is by revered teacher *Bhadrayana (vyasa)* and *bhashya* (commentary) by revered teachers like *Adi Shankracharyya* etc.

Numerous attempts were made in past on establishing *vedantic* philosophy at various times are

- *Shankracharyya* (8th century CE) – *Advita* (monism) - both the individual self (*Atman*) and Brahman are the same, and knowing this difference causes liberation, his commentary or *bhashya* on *prasthantri* is most reliable means of study of *vedanta*
- *Ramanujacharyya* (12th century CE) – *Vishista advita* (Qualified monoism) - all diversity is subsumed to a unified whole
- *Madhavacharyya* (13th century CE) – *Dvaita* (Complex dualism) - *Brahman* and *Atman* as two different entities, and *Bhakti* as the route to eternal salvation
- *Vallabhacharyya* (16th century CE) – *Sudh advita* (Pure monoism) - God and the individual self are the same, and not different.
- *Nimbarkachayya* (16th century CE) – *Dvaita – advita* (Dualism and monoism combined) - Brahman is the highest reality, the controller of all.
- *Chitanya, Rupa and Jiva Goswami* (16th century CE) -*Achintya bheda – abheda* (inconceivable difference and non-difference simultaneously

BHAGWATGITA

(Smriti prasthan)

Bhagwatgita or Gita is the sixth section of *Bhism parv* of *Mahabharta* which is epic composed by sage *Ved Vyasa*, Gita has 700 verses divided in 18 chapters.

It is a dialogue between lord *Krishna* and *Arjuna* who was lamenting at the battlefield of *Kuurkshetra* over fighting on *Dharam yudh* (war of righteousness) with their dear ones between Kaurva and *Pandavas.*

Krishna not only explains righteousness and duty to *Arjun* but also touches various aspect of brahman and revels various form of *yoga* and means to attaining brahman and liberation.

Chapter 1 – Dejection of *Arjun*

In the battlefield of *Kurukshetra* when armies of *Kauravs* and *Pandavs* were standing facing each other and ready for battle, *Arjun* asked his charioteer *Krishna* to take his chariot between the armies to asses' peoples, whom he need to engage in battle and arrangement of battlefield arrayed in front of each other.

Inspecting the arrangement of battlefield he finds his elders, nears & dears on eighter side of armies, he lamented by seeing that, and his mind got agitated in grief and casted off his bow to sank in hinder part of chariot, saying "I do not covet victory, nor kingdom or any pleasure even his life, I cannot hope to be happy by killing our own people and sin will surely occur to me." I do not want to kill them, though they may slay me, even for sovereignty over three world, further expressed that age old family traditions disappear with the destruction of family and having lost virtue, vices take hold of entire family race, and it is known that one whose family tradition is lost, dwells in hell for indefinite period of time, though we all possess intelligence but have set our mind on committing great sin and it is due to lust of throne and enjoyment by killing our own kinsmen.

Chapter 2 – *Shankhya Yoga* (Path of knowledge)

Krishna tried to persuade *Arjun* saying such act does not suit to noble men at this hour, but *Arjun* was adamant not to fight with his revered elders and further stating it is better to live on alms then killing, even after killing we will be left with blood-stained pleasure in form of wealth. *Arjun* continues saying that my mind is puzzled in regard to my duty, and I beseech you, please tell me decidedly what is good for me, I am your disciple please instruct me, I take refuge in you and *Arjun* became silent.

Krishna smiled and spoke

- You grieve over issue which one should not grieve and talk like learned person, wise men do not sorrow over dead or living, there was never a time when you, I and all these kings was not there nor hereafter cease to be existing, soul attains another body after childhood, youth and old age, so wise men does not delude about this.

- Endure feeling that, what comes in contact with senses and outer object gives feeling as hot and cold, pleasure and pain are all transitory and fleeting, wise men become eligible for immortality when he sees pleasure and pain alike and not tormented by object of contacts.

- Unreal has no existence and real never cease to be, reality of both is perceived by sear of truth, an attempt to know imperishable and indestructible which pervades this universe are both ignorant, who consider soul can be killed or are killed since it is imperishable, unborn, eternal, everlasting and primeval hence body is slain, and soul is not.

- As men sheds worn out garments and takes new one, like wise embodied soul casting off worn out body, enters new one. No weapon can cut, nor any fire can burn, water cannot wet, and air cannot dry the soul, it is eternal, pervading, immortal, constant and everlasting, it is unmanifested, incomprehensible and immutable, by knowing such form of soul one should not grief.

- Even if you consider soul as subject of constant death and rebirth, then also you should not grief since death is certain who is born and rebirth is inevitable, hence no point in lamenting on inevitable things, prior to birth and after death there are no senses as soul is unmanifested, it is only during interim period of manifestation one has senses and soul dwelling in bodies of all can never be slain, therefore you should not mourn for anyone.

- Consider your duty, as warrior your duty is to fight righteous war and it open gateway to heaven for you and by refusing to it, it will lead to loss of your reputation and will incur sin and undying infamy which is worst then death, in war if you die, it will win you heaven and if conquered you will enjoy sovereignty on earth, treat victory & defeat, gain & loss, pleasure & pain alike and prepare yourself for battle.

- In *karam yoga* or selfless action, there is no loss of effort, no fear of contrary result and intellect is determinate and firmly focused on goal.

- Ignorant people looks upon heaven as supreme goal and recommend many rituals for attainment of pleasure and power with rebirth as fruit, these people cannot attain determinate intellect connected to God, *vedas* deals with evolute of three *gunas or* qualities that is mode of *praktri* or nature for worldly enjoyment and modes of attaining it, but people rising above from pair of opposite (pain & pleasure etc.) which is established in eternal existence (God) and this self-controlled person understands brahman and find hardly any use of *vedas.*

- One has only rights to perform his duties and not on the outcome of action, do not consider yourself as cause of outcome at the same time do not consider inaction also.
- Evenness of mind is called *yoga*, performing your duty as established and by renouncing attachment to its outcome, and with even mindedness in success or failure. Action done with selfish motive is inferior in form, it is without equanimity or equipoise of mind and people performing such work only for the fruit are like beggars. Wise men having equipoised mind and renouncing fruits of action are freed from shackles of birth and attains blissful supreme state.
- Mind having crossed mire of delusion will grow indifferent to enjoyment of this world which are known or yet to be known and intellect not confused with conflicting statements, rest steady and undistracted on God and attains *yoga* (union with God).

Arjun asked, "what are sign of God realized soul with mind stable and established in *samadhai* or deep meditation, and in what way these kinds of men speak, sit, walk etc."

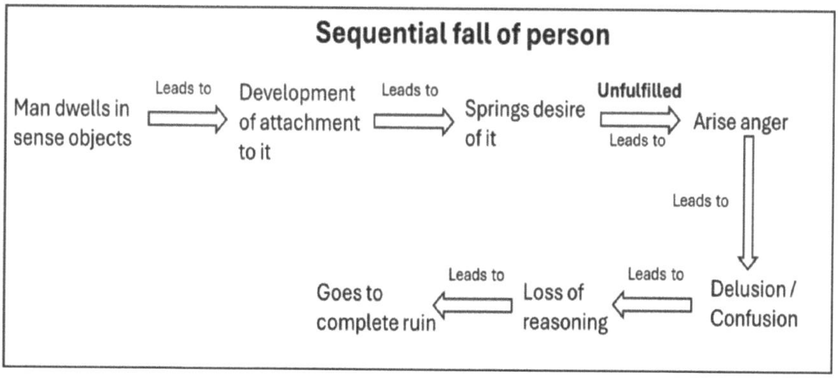

Krishna replied, one who cast off all cravings of mind and is satisfied in itself, who is in all joy to self and mind remain unperturbed in sorrow, its thirst for pleasure disappeared, unattached to everything and free from passion, fear or anger, like tortoise withdrawing all senses from the sense objects, at this point sense objects turns away from him as it does not enjoy them.

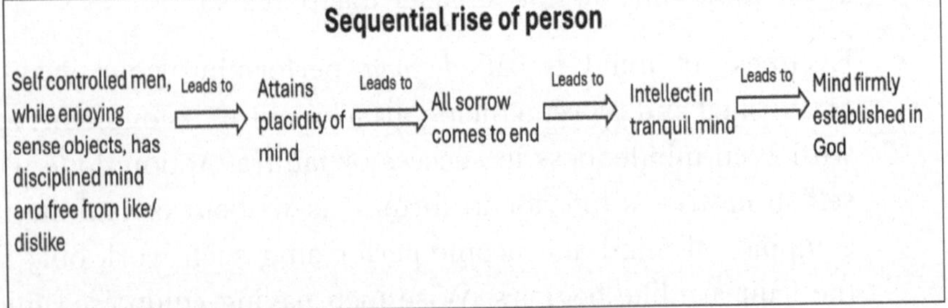

'Senses by nature is turbulent, even wise men are carried away by them, but having controlled all senses and by

concentrating mind, by devoting himself, its heart and soul to God becomes stable in mind.

As the ocean remains undisturbed when water from different rivers enters it, likewise when all enjoyment merges themselves without disturbing a tranquil mind, one who has given up all desires, egoism and thirst for enjoyment attains peace.

Chapter 3 -*Karma yoga* (Path of action)

Arjun asked, "it is considered knowledge is superior to action, then for what reason you urge me to perform dreadful action, my mind is puzzled with conflicting expressions, please tell me definitively."

Krishna said, there are two courses of *sadhana* or spiritual discipline which are *Sankhya yoga* and *karma yoga*, one cannot attain freedom from action without entering in action and cannot reach perfection of knowledge by ceasing to act.

One cannot remain without action even for a moment and is helplessly driven to action by *prakrti* or nature and anyone who is outwardly restraining the senses to the sense objects, is with deluded intellect and is hypocrite, on the other hand one who controls senses and action by their will power and remains unattached while undertaking selfless action excels, hence do your allotted duties and action is superior to inaction without action you cannot even maintain your body.

Man is bound by his own action hence perform your duties efficiently, which should be free from attachment as we perform *yagya's* (presented in *vedas* as duty to God). *Bhrama* (creator) after creating mankind made arrangement to foster God's through yagya's or sacrifices and let God foster you, and by fostering each other selflessly both attain highest good.

One who does not follow the wheel of creation and does not perform assigned duty leads to sinful and sensual life, however one who takes delight in self alone and gratified with self, contend with self has no duty, since he has nothing to gain by action or abstaining from action and does not have selfish dependence on any other creature. Perform your duty efficiently all the time without attachment to it, in this way wise men reach perfection which is important for worldly order also.

Actions performed by great people are imitated by others and, it sets benchmark for them, so I (God) have no duties to perform in any of three world as nothing to be attained by me, but still I continue to work, if ever I cease to work, world will perish, so to maintain world order I act without attachment to it.

Wise men established in self should not unsettle mind of ignorant, who is attached to action but should guide them to perform their selfless duties while performing his own duty.

All actions are performed by modes of *prakriti* or nature but fools, whose mind is deluded by egoism thinks "I am the doer", he who has true insight in sphere of *guna* (quality, which is mode of *praktri*) and their actions, holding in *guna* (senses, mind etc.) and moves among the *guna* of object does not gets attached to it, hence dedicate all actions to me (God) with mind fixed on me, free from desire and feeling of "Meum et Tuum" and cured with mental coagulation.

If asked that all living creatures follow their natural instinct, even wise men act according to their tendencies, then there should be no use of restraining by force, but the basic sense of attraction and repulsion are rooted in all sense- object hence man should never allow himself to be swayed by them and attraction and repulsion are two main enemy in the way of redemption.

One's own duty though devoid of merits is preferable then the duty of another's well performed work, even death is performing his duty is bliss for him, but another's duty is fought with fear by us.

Arjun asked, "which force impels one to commit sin, in some case involuntarily."

Hierarchy of self

Gross body < Senses < Mind < Intellect < Self

By knowing self, one can kill enemies, which are in form of desires difficult to overcome

Krishna replied, Desire born from *Rajas guna* is wrath and is insatiable, wicked and enemy to us, it is like smoke which surrounds fire or dust covering mirror, in same way knowledge is covered by desire and embodied soul is covered by senses, mind and intellect.

One must first control senses and then kill other evil things which is obstruction to knowledge of absolute or *Nirguna* brahman (without qualities) and *vijnana* (manifested divinity).

Chapter 4 – *Jnana yoga* (Knowledge and discipline of action)
Arjun asked, "how can I belive that you imparted *yoga* at the beginning of creation, since you are contemporary to me and sun-God dates back to time primordial."

Krishna replied, you and I have passed through many births in past, I remember all of them and you do not, though I am birthless, immortal and lord of all being, still I manifest through my *yogmaya* or divine illusion to keep my nature under check.

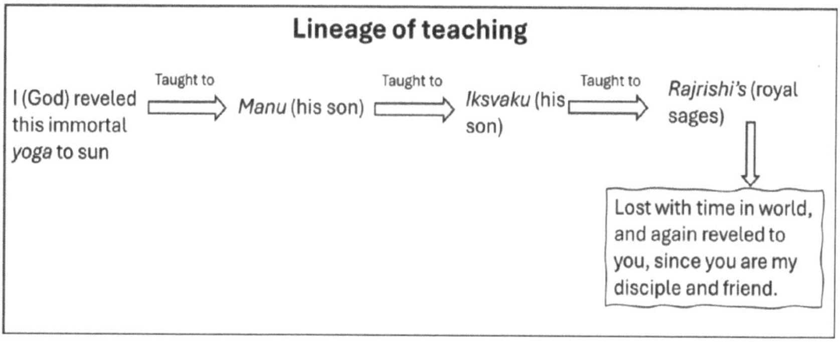

Whenever righteousness is on decline and unrighteousness is on ascendent, I (God) enbody myself forth for protection of virtious and expiration of evil doers and to establish dharma on firm footing at every age of humanity, my (God) birth and activity is divine, he who knows this is not reborn and comes to me, many has become part of me in past, they were completely rid of attachments, fear and anger and purified by the penance of wisdom.

Order of society is created by me, classifying based on *guna* or quality of nature predominent in each one of them and appropiating duties are assigned to them, though creator (me) is non-doer have no craving for the fruit of action so the fruit of action does not taint me, he who knows me in this way is not bound by fruits of action, having known this ancestors performed their assigned duties accordingingly, so you also do your assigned duties as they did in past.

Even wise men are puzzled with, what is action and what is inaction, so I expound you truth about action, by knowing this, it will free you from evil effects and sackles of *karma*, first we must understand action, inaction and prohibated action.

- He who see action in inaction and inaction in action is a wise men, his undertaking are free from desire and *sankalp* (thought of world), it's fruits of actions are burnt up by fire of wisdom.
- He who has given up attachment to action and fruits of it, no longer depends on anything in the world and is ever content, so he does nothing at the same time fully engaged in action.
- Having subdued his mind and body, given up all enjoyments and free from craving while at the same time performing actions bodiely, does not incur any sin.
- *Karmyogi* (selfless action) is one who is contended with whatever he gets unsoughted and is free from jealousy, all pairs of opposite (joy & greif etc.) are not bound by his actions.

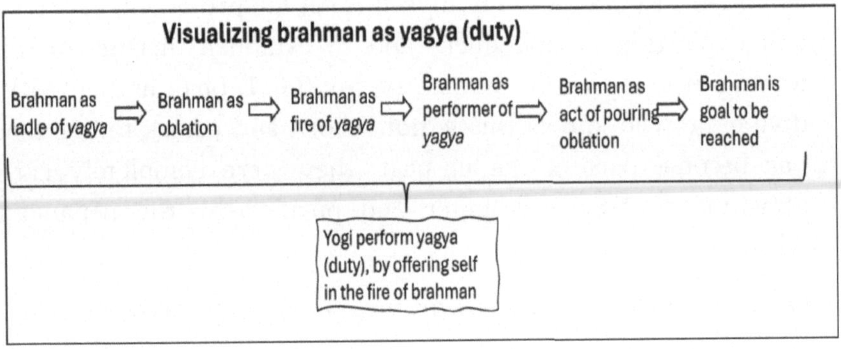

- One who is free from attachment with no identification of himself with body, free from feeling of mine and yours, mind transfixed in knowledge of self and works merely for the sake as *yagya* or duty for such people all fruits of actions gets dissolved entirely.
- Practice for seeing brahman everywhere as form of *yagya* or duty
- Some sacrifice their sense of hearing, sound and other senses in the fire of self discipline and other sacrifice with material possessions, some offer sacrifice in form of austerity and vows,

some perform sacrifices by wisdom through study of sacred text, some *yogi's* offers inhalations into that of exhalation or vise-a-versa, some perform *pranayam* with regulated diet and breathing, to them all of these their sins are consumed and all of them understand meaning of sacrificial worship, *yogis* enjoy nector leftover after sacrifice to attain brahman and one who do not offer sacrifice in this world is not happy here and other world also.Many such form of sacrifices is set forth in *vedas* in detail, know them all as action of mind, body and senses, sacrifice through knowledge is superior to all other sacrifices, since all other culminates to knowledge and it is with no exception.

To understand true knowledge, it is by approaching sear of truth with salutation at their feet, render them services and question them with open and guileless heart, when you achieve elightment then ignorence will delude you no more, in the light of knowledge you will see entire creation first within yourself and then in others, with this knowledge even most sinful of sinner is freed like blazing fire eats up all fuel.

According to spirit of *karmyoga* or selfless duty, action do not bind him who has dedicated all his actions to God, therefore slashing to pieces with sword of knowledge and doubt in heart born out of ignorence and establish yourself in *karamyoga.*

Chapter 5- *Karamsansya yoga (Yoga* of knowledge and action)

Arjun asked, "you extol *shankhya yoga or yoga* of knowledge and then *karm yoga or yoga* of action, please tell me decidely what is appropiate to me."

Krishna said, *karamyoga* or yoga of selfless action and *sanyasyoga* or yoga of knowledge both leads to supreme bliss, however yoga of action is earier to practice and superior to yoga of knowledge. *Karamyogi*, neighter hates nor desires is considered renunciation which is free from pair of opposite (happiness or pain) is liberated from the bondage while igonerant says *shankhayayoga* and *karamyoga* leads to different outcome, however one firmely established in eighter gets fruit of both which is God realization.

Shankhayayoga which has doer ship in relation to mind, senses and body is difficult to accomplish, whereas *karamyogi* keeps his mind transfixed in God reaches brahman soon, *karamyogi* who has conquered his mind and mastered his senses with pure heart and identifies himself with self in all being are not tainted while performing action, *karamyogi* performs action only with their senses, mind, intellect and body without feeling of mine and shaking off attachment, does action only for purification and offering fruit of action to God and attain everlasting peace in the form of God realization.

Shankhayogi does nothing or gets nothing done by others and remains in bliss by relinquishing all actions, its mind and intellect is totally merged in God and establishes identity with him and eventually becomes one with self, its sins are wiped out by wisdom and reaches supreme goal, whence there is no return and looks with equanimity in all eighter its brahman, cow, elephant, dog or pariah.

Pleasure born of sense- contents are source of suffering which appears enjoyable to world minded people and it has beginning and an end are fleeting, so wise men do not indulge in them, he who understand this in present life or before casting off this body about urgers, lust and anger is a *yogi* and a happy man, he is happy within himself and enjoys within himself the delight of soul, such person is *shankhyogi* who is identified with brahman is at all peace by shutting out all thoughts of external enjoyment with gaze fixed between eye-brows, having regulated breath and have brought senses, mind and intellect under control and free from desire, fear and anger is liberated.

Chapter 6 – *Atman sanyas yoga or Dhyan yoga (Yoga* of self-control)

One who does his duty without expecting fruit of action is *sanyasi* or renunciant and *karamyogi* or with selfless action both, just by giving up sacred fire or worldly action one does not become *sanyasi* or giving up all activity one does not become *yogi*, since *sanyasi* and *yogi* are same and anyone abandoning *sankalp* or thought of world are not *yogi* but when men ceases to have attachment to object of senses and action, and have renounced all *sankalp* is said to have attained as *yogi* and he is friend with his soul and lower self (mind, senses and body) conquered, otherwise it is enemy to the self. Supreme self is rooted in self-controlled men, whose mind is perfectly serene in pair of opposite (cold and heat, joy or sorrow, honor and ignominy etc.).

Arjun asked, "mind by nature is restless, hence I do not perceive stability in this *yoga* in form of equanimity and I find difficult to control mind as in case of wind."

Krishna replied, "no doubt that mind is restless and difficult to control but can be brought in control with practice and exercise of dispassion." *Yoga* is difficult to achieve by one whose mind is not subdued by him, however it is possible with mind under control and ceaselessly striving for it through practice.

Arjun asked, "what is destiny of aspirant who endow with faith in *yoga* but is not able to subdue his passion of mind, therefore is diverted from *yoga* at the time of death, since he has failed to reach perfection is deprived of both God realization and enjoyment of sense-objects."

Krishna replied, there is no fall for him in eighter case here or thereafter for one who strives for redemption and never meets evil destiny.

- Having stayed with *yoga* till death, shall obtain higher world (heaven) and stay there for long and reborn again among virtuous people
- Otherwise, possessed of dispassion are born in family of enlightened *yogi's,* which is difficult to obtain, he auto regains latencies of even mindedness of previous birth and strive harder for perfection and some take birth in rich families and swayed away from senses and feels drawn toward God by force of habits acquired in previous birth.

However, one who diligently takes up practice in this life will attain perfection with latencies acquired in many previous births.

Chapter 7 – *Jyana vijyan yoga* (material and spiritual of absolute)

Entirety of wisdom of God in his absolute is 'formless" state along with qualified aspect of God, one among the thousand strive to realize me (God) and among these striving some rare one devoting himself entirely to me, knows me.

My lower nature (material part) is in eight parts which are earth, water, fire, air, ether (space), mind, intellect and ego (self-consciousness) and my higher nature (spiritual) is in form of *jiva* (life principle) by which entire universe is sustained. All being evolved from these two-fold *praktr*i or nature, and I am the source of entire creation, it is like cluster of yarn bead formed by knot on thread. Whatever other entities are born of *sattva* or goodness, *rajas* or activity and *tamas* or inertia are all evolved from me, in reality neither do I exist in them, nor they do in me. Entire creation is deluded by these objects evolved from three modes of *praktri (sattva, rajas* and *tamas*), world fails to recognize me as, I stand apart from these creation and *maya* or illusion constituting of *gunas* or qualities is extremely difficult to break through, however those who constantly adore me are able to cross it, others whose wisdom carried away by *maya* or illusion are of demonic in nature and such fools do not adore me.

Four types of devotees with noble deeds, they worship me are

- Seeker after worldly possessions
- Afflicted
- Seeker of knowledge
- Person with wisdom

Among them best is man with wisdom, who has established identity in me, however all these are noble.

Wisdom if carried away by various desires and prompted by their own nature, they worship other deities by adopting norms relating to each celestial form, devotee craving for worldly objects choses to worship with their own reverence, but I (God) stabilize faith of such devotee in that form to obtain desired enjoyment through that deity as ordained by me, however fruits gained by these understanding are perishable.

Veiled by my *yogmaya* or divine potency, I (God) do not manifest to all and ignorant do not recognize me and consider me as subject of birth and death, however those who take refuge in me and strive for deliverance, comes to know *brahman* or absolute, *adhyatma* or embodied soul, *karma* or action and my integral being which is *adhibhuta* or field of matter, *adhibhava* or brahma and *adhiyajna* or unmanifested.

Chapter 8 – *Aksharapara brahmyoga (yoga* of indestructible brahman)

Arjun asked, what is brahman (absolute), *Adhyatma* (spirit), Karma (action), *Adhibhuta* (matter) and *Adhidaika* (divine intelligence), further who is *Adhiyajna* (unmanifested divinity dwelling in heart of all being) and how to realize it.

Krishna replied, He who departs body thinking of me (God) attains to me, otherwise thinking of whatever entity at the time of leaving body that one is attained, he is eventually absorbed in his thoughts, hence think of me all the time and perform your assigned duty.

- *Brahman* – supreme indestructible
- *Adhyatma* – individual soul
- *Karma* – primal resolve of God also known as *Visarga*, which is existence of being.
- *Adhibhuta* – all perishable objects
- *Adhidaiva* – shining purusha also brahman
- *Adhiyajna* – myself (God) dwelling in body as inner witness

One Brahma day is one thousand *mahayuga* (4,32,000 human years comprising of *sat, traita, dwapar* and *kali* yuga) is reality of time, all embodied being emanates from unmanifested at the beginning of cosmic day and merges back into same subtle body at cosmic nightfall and beyond this there is an another unmanifested existence that is supreme divine being, who do not perish when all is perished and it is indestructible are called supreme God and this is in my abode, by attaining which one do not return to mortal world.

Time and path of departing soul which do not return and time and path of departing soul to return back to mortal world is discussed now.

One dying in period of, which fire God (sun) and deities presiding over daylight of "*shuklapaksha*" (15 days of bright lunar fortnight) and God of "*uttrayan*" (6 months of solar summer solstice) are in path which leads to brahman, not to return, wherein God presiding over smoke, in "*krishnapaksha*" (15 days of dark lunar fortnight) and God of "*Dakshinnayan*" (6 month of solar winter solstice) is the path led by Gods one after another to attain luster of moon (symbolic to enjoying fruits of good deed in heaven) and return to mortal world after that.

Realizing this truth, transcends all reward enumerated in *veda* as performance of *vagya* or sacrifice, austerities and charity to attain supreme and primal state.

Chapter 9 & 10 – *Rajvidya rajghru & Vibhuti yoga* (yoga of sovereign science and yoga of divine manifestation)

Most secret knowledge of *nirgun brahman* or without qualities along with knowledge of manifest divinity of *nirgun* and *sagun* or with quality is sovereign science, sovereign secret, supremely holy, excellent, enjoyable, is attained by virtue and easy to practice.

Entire universe is permeated by me (God) as unmanifested divinity, all dwells within me but I am not present in them, all being do not abide in me but behold power of my divine yoga as sustainer and creator of being, as wind blowing everywhere remains in sky, likewise all being originated from my *sankalp or* resolution abide in me and at the time of dissolution of world, all being enters in my *prakrti or* nature/ prime cause and at the beginning of creation, I send them forth again.

I create again and again according to one's *karma,* however by doing so, such action it do not bind me and under my aegis, nature brings entire creation of both sentient and insentient being, by this cause wheel of *samsara* or cycle of birth and death goes around.

Those performing action with some motives as laid down in *vedas* and worshiping me through *yagya* or sacrifices seeks access to heaven and attains *Indra's* (King of God) paradise as result of virtuous deeds and they enjoy celestial pleasure of heaven, and they return to mortal world on stock of their merit being exhausted. However, one who constantly thinks of me, worship me in disinterested spirit and remains united with me through thoughts, to them I bring full security and personally attend their needs, it is same even to those devotees who endowed with faith and worship other God with same interest and motive worship me, though with mistaken approach. Those who votaries God goes to God, those who votary manes reach manes, those who adore spirit reaches to spirit and those who worship me comes to me and freed from cycle of birth and death.

Arjun asked, by what process, I can know you and in what form you to be meditated upon, you alone can describe in full your own glory, whereby you pervade in entire world.

Krishna replied, there is no limit to my manifestation, I am universal self, seated in heart of all beings, I am beginning, middle and the end of all beings, I hold entire universe by fraction of my *yogic* power.

Chapter 11- *Vishwarupa sandarshan yoga (yoga* of vision of cosmic body)

Arjun asked, I long to see your divine form possessed of wisdom, glory, energy, strength, valor and effulgence, if you think that can be seen by me, then o' lord revel to me your imperishable form.

Krishna replied, you cannot see me with your physical eye, therefore I give you divine eyes with this behold my glorious divine power of yoga.

Krishna then revealed his supremely glorious divine form, having many mouths, eyes, wonderful sight with many divine ornaments, divine weapons, divine garland, anointed with divine fragrance, with infinite number of faces in all direction and was illuminated as of thousand suns bursting forth at once.

Arjun asked, as moth rushes with great speed into blazing fire for extinction out of *moha* or illusion, same way all warriors of mortal world is entering in your flaming mouth to meet their doom, tell me who are you, be kind to me, I wish to know you, I am not able to understand your nature.

Krishna replied, I am mighty *kaal or* time/ destroyer of world, I am here to exterminate these people, even without you fighting and killing them, hence arise and win glory by conquering foes and enjoy affluent kingdom, all these warriors are already slain by me, you are just an instrument.

Arjun asked, having seen your wondrous form, I feel transported with joy and at the same time I am tormented with fear, I pray, please revel me your divine form of *Vishnu or* principal God.

Krishna replied, in this mortal world, I cannot be seen in this form by anyone other than you, it is not possible by study of *vedas* or by any rituals, gift, actions, austere, penances and do not be perturbed or perplexed by it, however with fearless and tranquil mind behold once again four armed form of mine, then he reveled to *Arjun* his four armed form and consoled frightened *Arjun* and said this form is difficult to behold, even to God's but with single minded devotion, I can be seen in this form of *Vishnu.*

Chapter 12 – *Bhakti yoga (yoga* of devotion)

Arjun asked, between two forms of worship, who is best knower of *yoga*, one who is constantly devoted to you in manner stated earlier, or other who adore you as supreme reality as indestructible, unmanifested brahman.

Krishna replied, it is strenuous for those who have their mind attached to unmanifested, as it is difficult for body conscious people, however people depending on me and surrendering all actions to me, then I speedily deliver from the ocean of birth and death.

If one cannot steadily fix mind on me, then seek to attain me through practice, if you are not able to pursuit such practice then intent to work for me alone, by that you shall attain perfection, if you are unable to do this also then subduing your mind and intellect by relinquishing fruit of all action.

Knowledge is better than practice of discrimination, meditation to God is superior to knowledge and renunciation of fruit of action is superior to meditation which gives peace immediately.

Order of superiority of yoga

Renunciation of fruit of action > Meditation to God > Knowledge > Practice without discrimination

Chapter 13 – *Kshetra, kshetrjna vibhag yoga (yoga* of discrimination between *kshetra* (residence) and knower of *kshetra or kshetrjna*)

Body is termed as field or *kshetra* and knower of the field is *ksherjna*, true knowledge is knowing of the field, it is elaborated in different *vedic* texts and conclusively told in *brahmasutra.*

Khestra is five elements which are ego or self-consciousness, intellect, unmanifested matter, ten organs of perception and mind with five object of senses (sound, touch, color, taste and smell) along with desire, aversion, pleasure, pain, physical body, consciousness and firmness, are ought to be known by which one attains supreme bliss (brahman), who is lord of two beginningless entity *prakrti* or nature) and *jiva* or individual soul.

Prakrti and *jiva* is neither *sat* or being) nor *asat* or nonbeing, though pervading in all sense object, but is devoid of all senses and not attached to anything.

All objects constituted of *guna* or qualities of like, dislike etc. are born of *praktri* or nature and is said to be responsible for bringing forth evolutes and instrument to it, while *purusa* or individual soul is responsible for experience of joy and sorrow etc., *purusha* in association with *praktri* experiences object of nature by three *gunas or* qualities, which are evolved from *praktri* itself and is responsible for birth of soul in good or evil womb.

Sprit dwelling in individual body is same as supreme self and is witness, guide, sustainer and experiencer simultaneously. He who knows *purusha* or individual soul and *prakriti* or nature along with three *gunas* or qualaties and performing his duty in every way is not born again.

Some by meditation behold spirit in heart with help of sharp intellect and others through discipline of knowledge and some by discipline of action (*karamyoga*) but he who sees as action is performed by *praktri* or nature and self as non-doer actually sees reality. Indestructible sprit dwelling in body does nothing nor is tainted by any action, as sun illuminates entire universe but is not tainted by any of it, so as *atma* or individual soul illuminates entire *khestra* or field, those who perceive this with eyes of wisdom the difference between *khestra* and *khestrjana*, the phenomenon of liberation from *praktri* or nature and their evolutes, reaches the external sprit or brahman.

Chapter 14 – *Gunatrai vibhag yoga (yoga* of division of qualities of *prakriti*- nature) -

Binding of " Individual soul" to body, by *gunas* (qualities) of *prakriti* (nature)

Gunas (quality)	Properties	Binds "individual soul" to body by
Sattva	Immaculate is illuminating and flawless	Happiness and knowledge
Rajas	Passion born from desire and attachment	Action and their fruit
Tamas	Deluder, looks upon body as own self, ignorant	Error (procrastination), sloth and sleep

Sattva or goodness, *Rajas or* passion and *Tamas* or darkness) are three *gunas* or qualities born of *prakriti* or nature, it is responsible for tying individual soul or *atman* to body.

Person with predominance of "*guna*" (quality)

Overpowered *guna*	Prevailing *guna*	Characteristic of person
Rajas and *Tamas*	*Sattva*	Light of discernment drawn in body, mind and senses
Sattva and *Tamas*	*Rajas*	Greed, activity, action with motive , restlessness and thirst for enjoyment
Sattva and *Rajas*	*Tamas*	Obtuseness of mind and senses, disinclination to perform obligatory duty

Person dying with predomenence of *sattva guna,* obtains eternal world or heaven etc. while dying with predominence of *rajas guna* is born among people attached to action and dying with predominence of *tamas guna* is born in speices of deluded creatures as insects, beast etc.

Reward for righteous act is *sattva guna,* sorrow is the fruit of *rajas guna* and ignorence is fruit of *tamas guna.*

Person who sees performer of all activities are these three *gunas,* and realize me (God) as supreme self standing beyound *gunas* as obsever only, enters in my being and having transcended three *guna* are freed from birth, death, old age and all kind of sorrow.

Arjun asked, what are the marks of one who has risen above three *gunas or* qualities and how he conducts and what are the ways he has risen above three *gunas.*

Krishna replied, he who do not abhor anything and is illuminated is *sattva,* engaged in activity is *Rajas* and stupor is Tamas, such *gunas* or qualities when not prevalent and neither long for it and are ceased to be and acts as witnesses only and not disturbed by three *gunas* and always identify himself with God. He is ever established in self and takes pain and pleasure alike, regards clod of earth, stone and gold alike, equipoised in honor and ignominy and is alike for friends and enemies.

Chapter 15- *Purushottam yoga (yoga* of supreme person)

Eternal *Jivatam or* individual soul in body is fragment of my (God) own self, it draws around mind and five senses which is abide in *praktri* or nature with three *guna*, as wind waft scent, in same way *Jivatman* or individual soul takes mind and senses from body when it leaves body and takes along when it enters to another body.

I remain seated in heart of all creatures as inner controller and I the source of memory, knowledge through *vedas,* I the origin of *Vedanta* and power of *vedas,* I am perishable and imperishable too (being as perishable and Jivtaman as imperishable), hence I am (God) known as *Purushottam* or the supreme self in world and *vedas.*

Chapter 16- *Devasur sampad vibhag yoga (yoga* of discrimination between godly and demonic properties)

Born with divine endowment	Born with demonic properties
• Fearless, purity of mind, fixity of mind in meditation, charity in *sattvik* form, control of senses, worship of God/ deity/ elders, performance of *agnihotra* (daily rituals), study and teaching of *vedas* (duty) • Suffering hardship in discharge of obligation of duty, non-violence in action /thoughts/ word or deeds, truthfulness and geniality	• Hypocrisy, arrogance, pride, anger, sternness (obstinacy) • Impurity (external and internal), bad conduct • Thinks that world is without foundation and is not real and goodness brought forth by union of male and female

in speech, absence of anger, disclaiming doer ship, abstaining from slander, compassion, nonattachment to object of senses, sublimity, forgiveness, fortitude and absence of self-esteem. **Conducive for liberation**	• Clinging and inclination on destruction of world • Desire for material things and embracing false doctrine and conduct is impure • Care to self in innumerable ways and remain devoted to enjoyment of sensuous pleasure • Held in bondage of expectations, leading to anger • Lust for creating wealth by all means • Believes himself as mighty and happy • Intoxicated with wealth and self-conceited **Leading to bondage**

A person with demonic properties is born, life after life in demonic womb and verily sinks down to a lower plane.

Desire, anger and greed are gate to hell and bring downfall to the individual soul or *atman.* One who discards injunctions of scripture and acts in arbitrary ways to his own will can never attain occult powers nor supreme goal or happiness. Hence scriptures (*sastra*) are your guide in determining what should be done and what not to be done.

Chapter 17- *Shraddha vibhag yoga (yoga* of division of three kinds of faith)

Arjun asked, where do a person stand who disregard injunctions of scripture and worship of God.

Krishna replied, faith of men is of three kinds, *sattvik, rajas* and *tamas,* faith of men are in confirmation of material disposition, faith constitute men based on nature of their faith.

Practice	*Sattvik*	*Rajas*	*Tamas*
Worship	God	Demigods and demons	Spirit of dead and ghosts
Food	Promotes longevity, intelligence, vigor, health, happiness, cheerfulness which are juicy, succulent, substantial and naturally likeable	Bitter, sour, salty, extremely hot, pungent, dry and burning which causes suffering, grief and sickness	Ill- cooked, not ripened, Insipid, putrid, stale, polluted and impure
Sacrifices	As ordained by scriptural (*sastras*) injunctions, by not expecting anything in return and believes it to be performed as duty	Offered for the sake of showing off or with expectation of fruits	Not confirmatory with scriptural injunctions, in which no food is offered, or no fee is paid, done without sacred chants

			or hymns and devoid of faith
Penance – *tyag or* relinquishing	Done with supreme faith and expecting nothing in return • Body – worship to God, brahman, guru, elders, great soul with purity, straight forward, celibacy and non-violence • Speech - no annoyance to others, truthful, agreeable, beneficial, study of *vedas* and other sastras, practicing and chanting divine names • Mind – cheerfulness, placidity, contemplation	Performed for the sake of show off, honor or self-admiration, selfish gain eighter done sincerely or ostentation and yields uncertain or momentary fruits.	Resorted out of foolish obstinacy, self-harm to mind, speech and body, done with intention to harm others

	of God, control on thoughts, purity of inner feeling		
Charity	Bestowed with sense of duty, expecting nothing in return and done at appropriate time, place to appropriate person	Bestowed with grudging spirit, expecting favor in return or hope for obtaining reward	Done without good grace in disdainful spirit, which is out of time, place to not deserving person

OM, TAT, SAT is appellation to brahman, who is truth, consciousness and bliss, by which *vedas* as well as sacrifices are done in cosmic dawn.

OM – Divine name, *TAT* – All belongs to God, *SAT* – Sense of reality and goodness

Chapter 18 -*Moksha sanyasa yoga (yoga* of liberation through path of knowledge and surrendering self)

Arjun asked, I wish to know the truth of *sanyasa* or renunciation and *tyag* or relinquish

Krishna replied, *Sanyasa* is understood as giving up all actions which are motivated by desire and *tyag* is relinquishing fruits of all action and some believe that all actions contain measure of evil, hence it is worth giving up, while act of sacrifice (selfless action), charity and penance are not to be shred, as these acts are for purification to wise men and must be performed along with other act of duties without attachment and expectation of reward.Since all actions cannot be given up entirely by anyone possessing body, but one can renounce fruits of action are called *tyag*.

In *shankhya* or knowledge, five factors are mentioned as means of neutralizing all actions, these are body, performer, organs of different kinds and their function, *divya* or latencies of past action, with these five and "knowledge" with "object of knowledge" motivates action, while performer, organs and activity constitute action.

In branch of knowledge dealing with *praktri* or nature and their *guna* qualities or modes of *praktri*, knowledge, action and doer, each have three guans of *praktri* (*Sattva*, *Rajas* and *Tamas*), with predominance of any of it in them.

Trait	***Sattvik***	***Rajas***	***Tamas***
Tyag (relinquishing)	Performing prescribed duty and giving up attachment and fruit of action	Giving up duties for fear of physical strain	Abandoning prescribed duty out of ignorance
Knowledge	Perceive one as imperishable with divine existence and equally present in all being	Cognize many existences of various kinds, each apart from one another	Clings to own body as his entire world
Action	As ordained by scripture and not accompanied	Action which involves much strain	Action performed through sheer ignorance,

	by sense of being performer, action performed without attachment or aversion to outcome and seeks nothing in return	in performing and is performed for seeking enjoyment and it is full of egoism	without considering its consequences, these actions are for injuring others and is for own resourcefulness
Performance	Action is free from attachment, not egoism, endowed with zeal and remain un-swayed in success and failure	Full of attachment, seeking fruit of action, greedy, oppressive by nature and impure in conduct, it feels joy and sorrow from the action	Lacking purity, controlling actions, uncultured, arrogant, deceitful, inclined to rob others livelihood, slothful, despondent and procrastinating
Intellect	Able to correctly determine course of action, renunciation, clarity in	Does not perceive, *dharma* (good conduct) and *adharma*	Wrapped in ignorance, sees *adharma* as *dharma* and perceive things otherwise

	thought for ought to be done and what should not be done, fearless and directed for liberation	(bad conduct)	
Dhriti (firmness/ perseverance)	Controls function of mind, vital air (*prana*) and senses	Seeking reward of action, clutches fondness to virtues of earthly possessions and worldly enjoyments	Not giving up sleep, fear, anxiety and vanity
Joy	Enjoyment through practice of adoration, service to God etc, which appears as poison in beginning but is nectar at end, born from placidity of mind	By contact of senses with object of senses, is poison but appears as nectar	Stupefied self during enjoyment as well as at end of enjoyment, which is derived from sleep, indolence and obstinate error

	perfected by meditation on God		

Everyone in all three worlds is bonded by three *gunas* of *praktri (sattva, rajas* and *tamas)* and duty to all are assigned in accordance with to their innate mode of *prakrti* or nature with qualities *or guna.*

Person devoted to his own duty, attains highest perfection in form of God-realization, one's own duty though devoid of merit is better than duties of other, as its own duty is ordained by his own nature or *praktri* and it does not incur sin.

Process to attain actionless, highest consummation of *jyanayoga (*path of knowledge*)* and brahman

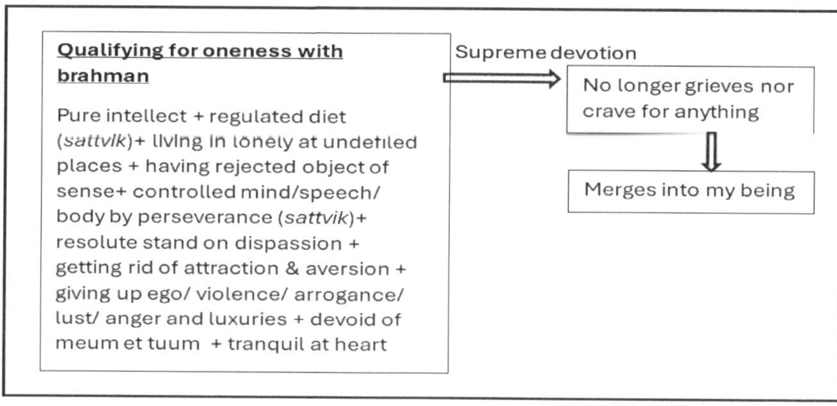

God abide in heart of all creatures, causing them to revolve according to their *karma* or action and by power of *maya* or illusion like machine mounted on them, this is most profound secret of all knowledge.

UPNISHAD

Shruti prasthana - Revelation

(Ten principle *upnishad*)

Traditionally upnishads have their place in *Aranyaks* and *Brahmanas* section of *vedas* except for *Ishavasya* (Part of Samhita), later *upnishad* got independent position but still are considered as part of any of the *vedas.*

It is difficult to establish exact number of *upnishads,* as all of the religious sect in past to establish their authority, had written book and called them *upnishad*, example an *Upnishad* was written during time of emperor *Abkhar* under his command, all sects claimed their text from S*hruti* or verbal knowledge passed through generations is considered reliable source of knowledge.

However, *Muktika Upanishad* referred as canon of 108 *upaniṣads,* it is dialogue between *Rama* and *Hanuman,* where *Rama* proposes to teach *Vedanta,* says, "even by reading one verse of any *upanishad* with devotion, one gets the status of union with me, which is hard to get even by sages". It mentions one hundred and eight *upnishads,* among them ten *upnishads* are considered important from the point of view of *vedantic* philosophy and another three are considered part of old *unpnishads* which are *"Shvetashvatata, Kaushitaki* and *Maitrayaniya"* and principal *upnishads* are

1. ***AITAREYA*** **– Master** ***Aitarey***
2. ***BRIHADARANYAKA*** **– Discussion in forest**
3. ***CHANDOGYA*** **– Keys of knowledge**
4. ***ISHAVASYA*** **– The lord**
5. ***KENAO*** **– At whose command**
6. ***KATHO*** **–** ***Kathak*** **branch of** ***veda***
7. ***TAITTIRYA*** **–** ***Taittirya*** **branch of** ***veda***

8. *MUNDAKA*– In the feet of monk
9. *PRASHNA* – Questions, elaboration of *Mundka upnishad*
10. *MANDUKYA* – Master *Mandukya*

AITAREYA- Master Aitarey

Chapter 1- Creation by supreme self

Creation of four world of cosmic person

In beginning was the *atman* alone (supreme reality, omniscient, omnipotent, free from any characteristic, eternally pure etc.) and nothing else that winked eighter sentient or insentient and he thought to create world and *atman* or supreme self being a material and efficient cause, he created following

- *Ambhah* – world of water bearing clouds, far from heaven
- *Mariachi* – world of solar rays, which is intermediate space
- *Mara* – world of mortals, earth
- *Ap* – world of water, under the earth

Creation from *Virat* - separated out	**Organ**	**Controlling deity of organ**
Mouth	Speech	Fire
Nostril	Breath (*Prana*)	Air
Eyes	Sight	Sun
Ears	Hearing	Quarters of space (directions)
Skin	Hairs (touch)	Plants & trees
Heart	Mind (*manas*)	Moon
Navel	*Apana* (Exhalation)	Death
Virile	Organ of generation	water

To create guardian of world (without which world will perish), he drew forth from water (like lump of clay) and gave shape of *Virat*, which is gross form of cosmic person and first manifestation and brooded or *Abhyatapat / tapas* and with austerity over the lump, creation happened along with associated organ and controlling deity

Deity	Abode
Fire	Organ of speech
Air	Sight
Quarter of space	Ears
Plants & trees	Hair
Moon	Mind entered in heart
Apana (exhalation)	Death entered navel
Water	Semen entered virile

Transition of cosmic power in human

Deities thus created fell into ocean (*samsara*) and creator subjected *virat* to hunger and thirst, deities then asked creator (*Atman*) to find abode for them where they will establish themselves and have food. Creator brought option of cow, horse which deities denied as not enough for them and finally brought person they agreed, creator commanded deities to take respective abode in person & they occupied respective places

Hunger and thirst could not find a space in person, creator told them, I assign you to all those deities and share with them their space. Creator (*Atman*) thought to himself, I have world and guardian of world, now let me create food for them, *atman* brooded over the water and then emerged food. And food thus created wished to flee away and *atman* tried to grasp it with various organs

Attempt to grasp food by	**Result**	**Consequences**
Speech	Could not	Otherwise, one would be satisfied by just uttering food
Breath	Could not	Otherwise, one would be satisfied by just smelling food
Eye	Could not	Otherwise, one would be satisfied by just looking food
Ear	Could not	Otherwise, one would be satisfied by just hearing food
Skin	Could not	Otherwise, one would be satisfied by just touching food
Mind	Could not	Otherwise, one would be satisfied by just thinking food
Virile	Could not	Otherwise, one would be satisfied by just emitting food
Apana (exhalation)	He could	Grasper of food is *vayu (prana)* & thus breath lives on food

Entrance of self in body - having created world, its guardian and food, lord thought how could aggregation of body and organ exist without me & how to enter and identify myself, definitely not through senses I have created.

Lord entered through the door (*vidriti*) which is by piercing the end at place where parting of hair ends as this is the place of bliss, *atman* thus embodied has three abode which is three conditions, which are waking, dreaming and sleeping.

Mystic name of self- existent self – having acquired characteristic of *jiva* (embodied self) as result of entering in body, he identified himself with body and felt as blind and deaf, but at last is awakened that what else but himself is embodied soul, while identified with body.

Chapter 2 – Three successive births of self

First birth – Germ (semen) which is vigor or *tejas* bears self in self

Second birth – Child born of self is the body of his father who substitute performing vitious deeds and having accomplished his duties and reached his age of departure from world.

Third birth – Father is born again as child, *Rishi or* sage *(Vamdeva)* has said while lying in womb I came to know all births of Gods and hundreds of stronghold as if made of iron which confined me, yet I burst through that like a hawk, thus endowed with knowledge and becoming one with supreme self on dissolution of body and obtains all desire in heavenly world and becomes immortal.

Chapter 3 – Pantheistic self

It is told by sage *Vamdeva* that "one which is self out of two, *prana* (vital breath transforming to various sense organs) enters through toes and other one (witness the sensation and remembers them) enters and leaves from the top of head through the opening".

Real atman is omniscient, but sense organs are not, real myself is *atman* or individual self, one which enters through head and for his experience and *prana* becomes various organs to experience object. Higher self (enters through top of head) is in heart (*buddhi* perception) which is consciousness (*Prajnanam*) not *prana* or vital breath which enters through toes and manifest as senses. Self who is pure consciousness or *prajnanam* is brahman conditioned with *upadahis* or adjunct superimposed on it as *Indra, Prajapati,* Gods etc, which is not real.

BRIHADARANYAKA - Discussion in forest

Chapter 1 – Meditation on horse and fire used in *Aswamedha yagya* and meditation on different part of hoarse bears the same result with symbolic horse, *Aswamedha* is imagined as *Prajapati* or creator itself.

Part of horse - Symbolic	Part of horse – Symbolic	Part of horse - Symbolic
Head – Dawn	Back – Heaven	Blood vessel – River
Eye – Sun	Belly – Intermediate region	Liver & lung – Mountain
Vital breath – Wind	Hoof – Earth	Hair – Herbs & tree
Open mouth – Fire	Sides – Four quarter	Foreparts – Rising sun
Trunk – Year	Ribs – Intermediate quarters	Hinder part – Setting sun
Limbs – Season	Joints – Month & half month	Yawn – Lightning
Feet – Day & night	Bones – Stars	Body shaking – Thunder
Flesh – Cloud	Food in stomach – Sound	Making water - Rain

Contemplation of sacrificial vessel (*Mahiman*) of gold and silver is day as golden cup in front of hoarse & night as silver cup behind the horse pointing out as western sea.

Racer of the hoarse is God, stallion and gandherva (celestial musician) as runner and demon as horse man.

Process of creation – In beginning there was nothing in universe and all was covered with death (*Hiranyagarbha*) and he desired to have mind and created mind, he worshiped himself and water was produced (*Arka* is process of creation of water with self-worship is known as fire is *Aswamedha yagya*), water or *Arka* was like forth on water and became solid earth, in process of doing so *Hirayangarbha (viraj/ Prana/ Prajapati)* got tired, fatigued and heated so the fire came out from it and so they divided it in three part sun, fire and air.

He desired of second self to be born of him, and he (death) brought union of speech with mind and seed was borne for a year and projected it by opening his mouth and the child cried *bhan* (sound of frightened being) due to *avidya* (ignorance), without which no embodiment (creation) is possible. Seeing the child frightened and crying and again by union of speech of mind he brought whatever there is like all *vedas*, meters, sacrifices, men, animals and it ate everything, therefore death is called *Aditi.*

Horse sacrifice (*Aswamedha*) symbolizes evolution of universe, where sacrificer should meditate on fire as *Prajapati* or creator as it was before manifestation of name and form, as pot before manifestation was clay.

***Udgitha* sung by**	**Pleasure for**	**Good for**	**Evil action**
Speech	All	Itself	Pierced to speak improper
Smell	All	Itself	Pierced to smell improper
Seeing	All	Itself	Pierced to see improper
Hearing	All	Itself	Pierced to hear improper
Mind	All	Itself	Pierced to think improper

As discussed in preceding section on combined effort of horse sacrifice (*Aswamedha*) along with meditation is source to identify ourselves from *Hirayangarbha* or death, now source of rituals and meditation is discussed.

Prajapati or creator has two type of son Gods (*devas*) and demon (*asura*), God were few and demons many and God thought to get rid of *asura* by sacrifice (*Joytishtoma*) by means of *udgitha* (part of *samveda* chanted at sacrifice in loud voice) and they all senses sang *udgitha* by their turn which had no desired consequences.

Having tested the deities (senses are called deities) controlling the organs, were incapable of securing desired results due to attachment to individual pleasure, at last they tried *udgitha* by vital breath or *prana* and evil could not pierce through and demons were scattered as cold of earth by stone hitting to it hence destroyed and Gods established, and demon perished.

Purity of vital breath or *Prana* may be contaminated since it is *atman* or individual self of various organs, death or evil is caused by identification of self with object due to ignorance for the enjoyment, death is result of attachment of organs to sense objects but is not affected to one who identify themselves with *prana* or vital breath.

Deity (symbolic of sense organs) took away death or evil to the end of the quarter (direction) and let no one go there or else will meet evil or death, apparently there is no end of the quarter but are referred to the region beyond which *vedic* knowledge does not prevails, through meditation on *prana* as the self , one rids oneself from sin, evil, death hence *prana* or vital breath is called destroyer of death.

Consequently

Organ of speech freed from death	Fire became immortal
Organ of smell freed from death	*Vayu* (air) became immortal
Organ of sight freed from death	Sun became immortal
Organ of hearing freed from death	Quarters (direction) became immortal
Organ of mind freed from death	Moon became immortal

All eating of food is done by vital breath or *Prana* and Gods or sense organs asked, "since all food is with you, please give us our share", and sat around *prana* to gain share of their food from him.

Vital breath or *prana* is called "*ayasa angirasa*" for its essence (*rasa*) of the limb (*anga*), since *prana* or vital breath is the essence of all its limbs (sense organs), hence meditate on *prana* or vital breath not on sense organ.

Prana or vital breath is self not only for body but also for *vedas*, one must have firm convection about this knowledge, he who has wealth of *saman* (vital breath) obtains wealth etc. edifying repetition or *abhyaroha* of hymn called *pavamanas*, priest or *prastotri* chants the *saman* at sacrificial rituals "lead me from unreal to real (death to immortality) from darkness to light (death to immortality)" and let sacrificer ask for a boon obtained by chanting it, wins world of *hirayangarbha* or first manifestation of supreme self for him, and to him there is no fear of being admitted into the world.

In the beginning of universe it was self or *Viraj* alone & he came to know "I" or *aham* and then was afraid to be alone (People are afraid when alone) but thought what to be afraid of when there is none (with second entity fear arises), now not afraid but unhappy to be alone and desired of mate and divided his body in two parts, male and female and from their union humans were born, then she hided herself one by one as cow/ mere/ she-ass/ one hoofed animal etc and he became counterpart of it each time and so they produced everything that exist in pair down up to ant. *Viraj* or supreme self, realized that I produced all this, and I am the creator (*Viraj* projection was not different from him, he himself was the world), and he (*Viraj*) rubbed back & forth to produce fire from its source (hand and mouth) & whatever is liquid he produced from semen and that all is universe.

Consequentially undifferentiated universe became differentiated by name and form, but the same self is in body of all till the tip of the nail, and he remains hidden in the body as razor in case or fire in source. People do not see self when viewed in parts (as organ of speech, sight etc.) which are merely his functions, whereas self is separate from all these, we need to meditate upon self only, self was brahman in beginning and it became all, who soever eighter God, seers or man has this enlightenment becomes brahman. Man, worshiping deities or sense organs thinking he and they are different is like animal to the Gods or sense organs, as many animals are at service to God, even one animal taken away causes anguish, so it is not pleasing to God when one knows the truth.

In the beginning was the brahman alone and being one he did not flourish and further projected cast hood and *dharma* or duty, people desirous of desired result performed their rituals according to their *dharma*, ignorant man identifying himself with its cast or duty at every stage of life, which is controlled by *dharma* thinks he has certain duty to the Gods or sense organs and dependent on them like animals, ignorant person is an object of enjoyment, so far he offers oblations and perform sacrifices are object of enjoyment to Gods or sense organs, so far he studies *veda* is an object of enjoyment to *rishis* of sage, so far he makes offerings to manes and desires children are object of enjoyment to manes, so far he gives food and shelter to man are object of enjoyment to men, so far he gives fodder and water to animals is an object of enjoyment to animals. As one wishes no injury to its own body, so all being wishes no injury to him who has this knowledge, by knowing brahman one can rid himself of the bondage of duty or *dharma* which makes him an animal, as it was under compulsion he takes up bondage of ritualistic work as he is helpless.

This universe is a triad of name, form and work

Name – speech is the source or *uktha,* all names arise from the common feature or *samana,* so it has common name.

Form – Eye is the source or *uktha* as one is perceived.

Work – Body is the source or *ukta* as one is perceived.

These three together are one, this body however immortal entity is covered with truth, which is vital breath or *prana, atman* or individual self, covered by subtle body is difficult to understand.

Chapter 2 – *Gargya* and *Ajatastru, brahman* as source of world

There lived a proud but eloquent man of *Gargya* family called *Balaki,* he went to king of *Kashi* called *Ajatasatru* and offered him to tell him brahman, and to his proposal king promised him one thousand cows

***Gargya* argument**	***Ajatasatru***	
	Response	**Consequence (limited outcome)**
Meditate *purusha* as sun	No, meditate sun as head of all being as resplendent	Meditator becomes head and resplendent
Meditate *purusha* as moon	No, meditate moon as white robed	Meditator and his progeny become abundant of soma or

	radiant *soma* or Nectar	nectar & never runs short of food
Meditate *purusha* as lightening	No, it's meditation on luminous only	Meditator and his progeny become luminous
Meditate *purusha* as *akasha* or space/ Ether	No, it's meditation on full and unmoving	Meditators become filled with progeny and cattle which never extinct
Meditate *purusha* as air	No, meditating him as *Indra* or king of Gods, who is irresistible and unvanquished army	Meditator becomes ever victorious and invincible
Meditate *purusha* as fire	No, it's meditation on him as forbearing	Meditator and its progeny become forbearing
Meditate *purusha* as water	No, it's meditation on him as agreeable	Meditator becomes agreeable, harmonious with scriptures
Meditate *purusha* as mirror	No, it's meditation on him as shining as sword or intellect	Meditator becomes shining with vigor and intellect
Meditate *purusha* as sound	No, it's meditation on him as life	Meditator reaches full age on death

Meditate *purusha* as quarter or directions	No, it's meditation on him sound and inseparable	Meditator gets companions and followers who never depart
Meditate *purusha* as shadow	No, it's meditation on him as death	Meditator reaches full age on death
Meditate *purusha* as self	No, it's meditation on him as self-possessed	Meditator and its progeny become self-possessed

Ajatasatru said "if that is all and by knowing this much, brahman cannot be known, since it has limited outcome"

Gargya approached king as disciple and king took him by his hand and rose, and both of them came to a man sleeping, they addressed sleeping man with name, but he did not wake up, then push sleeping man with hand again and again till he wakes up.

Having demonstrated that self or *Atman* is different than body, *Ajatasatru* explains when a fully conscious man falls asleep where does he goes and how he comes back, when fully conscious being goes in sleep or *Vijnanamaya*, it absorbs function of sense organ through its own consciousness and rest in self or *akasa* which is in heart and called *svapiti* or dream state and at this state, there are achievements according to its pleasure within his own domain, when same being goes in *susupti* or deep sleep he does not know anything, but when he returns back called *hita* has reached summit of happiness and that is the place where self or brahman rest.

Two forms of brahman – Brahman has two form which is gross and subtle, through the superimposition of this form on account of *avidya* or ignorance brahman is comprehended

1. Gross form – other than air and *akasha* or space/ ether and gross form are mortal, limited and definite
2. Subtle form – air and *akasha* or space, it is immortal, unlimited and indefinite

Distinction between gross and subtle is truth and adjunct of brahman, form of the person is like cloth dyed with turmeric or wool of gray sheep etc but brahman is not like this or not like that (*neti, neti*) for him there is no proper description and that is truth.

Discussion of *Yajnavalkya* and *Maitreyi* – *Yajanavalkya* sought consent from his wives *Maitreyi* and *Katyayani* for embracing life of renunciation, *Maitreyi* asked if world full of wealth belongs to me, then would I be immortal, *Yajnavalkaya* replied no and with further enquiry he explains

- Husband is loved not for the sake of him, but for the sake of self
- Wife is loved not for the sake of her, but for the sake of self
- Son is loved not for sake of him, but for sake of self
- Wealth is loved not for sake of wealth, but for sake of self
- The world is loved not for the sake of world, but for sake of self
- God is loved not for sake of God, but for sake of self
- Being loved not for sake of being, but for sake of self
- All are loved not for sake of all, but for sake of self

Therefore, it is self to be realized, and it is self to be heard and meditated upon, by realization of self all is known and reject one who knows him as different from self.

Any particular object in waking or dream state is perceived with intelligence only, like a particular note of drumbeat/conch/ *Vina* can only be grasped when general kind of sound of instrument is known.

Universe was brahman prior to manifestation and in continuance also, name and form are non-different from each other but are adjunct or *upadihis* of brahman or supreme self, once differentiated from brahman or supreme self, it is impossible to perceive indifference as fire not differentiated from smoke.

At the time of dissolution brahman or supreme self remains same as bubble or foam merges to water, hence brahman or supreme self is to be realized as pure intelligence as one and homogeneous, as lump of salt in water taste same, similarly all that comes out are from same reality and to be realized as consciousness.

Maitreyi became confused that attainment of brahman or supreme self as pure consciousness, one losses its own conscious, for which *Yajnavalkya* said, this much knowledge is enough, otherwise with duality one smells another, one hear another, one speaks to another, one thinks of another but when everything become self then there is nothing to be known from another, owing to which all is known hence know the knower.

Interdependence of created object – knowledge of brahman or supreme self is means of becoming all, and effect is mutual dependence.

Mutual dependence	**Immortal being (*atman* or Individual self)**
Earth ⟺ All being	Body
Water ⟺ All being	Semen
Fire ⟺ All being	Speech
Air ⟺ All being	Vital breath
Sun ⟺ All being	Eyes

Moon ⟺ All being	Mind
Quarters (direction ⟺ All being	Ears
Lightning ⟺ All being	Light of body, skin
Thunder cloud ⟺ All being	Sound
Dharma(righteousness) ⟺ All being	Control of body at aggregate and individual level
Truth ⟺ All being	Inherent to elements, body and organ
Mankind ⟺ All being	All species (sentient & insentient)
Cosmic body ⟺ All being	*Viraj* (embracing all bodies and organs of all species)

Self-individual and supreme which is devoid of discrimination is the ruler (king) of all being, as spokes fixed to felloes of wheel, so as all being, all Gods or sense organs, all world, all organs and all individual creatures are fixed to self, he is the lord who has made all creatures and supreme person or *purusha*, which entered the body and there is nothing which is not covered by him or pervaded by him.

Lord transformed himself in accordance with each form and for the sake of making him known.

Indra or king of Gods may yoke tens of thousands of horses but the *atman* by sense organ can yoke infinite, brahman is without consequent, without interior or exterior but is all pervading.

Chapter 3

Emperor *Janak* of *Videha* once performed a *Rajsuya yagya* (to which king offers alliances and proclaim himself as emperor) and gifts were freely distributed to all scholars from different countries assembled for the function.

Emperor then wished to know the most erudite scholar of *veda* for which he gathered one thousand cows each with ten gold coins tied between their horn but none of the scholar dared, however *Yajanavalkya* told his pupil to drive these cows to their place, other scholars seeing cows being driven became furious and challenged him and each scholar by turn questioned *Yajanavalkya*

Question	**Response - *Yajanavalkya***
Asvala	
• Everything is taken over by death, by what means sacrificer free himself from reach of death	• Through *hotri* priest (duty is to invoke God by recitation of *Rigveda*), since sacrificer speech is *hotri* where "fire" as the means of liberation
• Everything is taken over by day and night by what means sacrificer free himself from reach of day and night or liberation from solar time	• Through *adhvaryu* priest (duty is to prepare accessories for sacrifices and offer oblation by reciting *Yajurveda*), it is an eye of the sacrificer and eye is seen as means of liberation
• Everything is taken over by bright and dark fortnight, by what means sacrificer free themselves from reach of dark & bright fortnight or liberation from lunar time	• Through *udgati* priest (duty is to chant hymns of *samveda*) which is vital breath of sacrificer and is the mean of liberation

• Sky is without support, by what means sacrificer go to heaven	• Through *brahma* priest (who supervise sacrifice) with mind upon moon, is the sacrificer mind and is the mean of liberation
• How many *Rigveda* verses by *hotr*i used in today's sacrifice,	• Three, which are introductory, sacrificial and eulogistic
• How many oblations used by *adhvaryu* priest today and what sacrificer won through it	• Blaze upward – wins world of Gods, Blaze with great noise – wins world of manes, Blaze sinks down – wins world of man
• How many Gods *brahma* priest praised to protect sacrificer today and what did sacrificer won	• Only one, the mind which is infinite or *viswdeva* and thereby sacrificer won infinite world
• How many hymns of praise *udgatri* priest chant today, which are they and what sacrificer wins through it Thereby *Asvala* held its peace	• Three which are, Introductory or *prana* – Earth is won, Sacrificial or *apana* – sky is won, Eulogistic or *vyana* – heaven is won
Artabhaga • How many *grahas* or sense organs and *atigrahas* or object of senses are there	**Grahas** — **Atigrahas** *Prana*(nose) — *Apana* (odor) *Vak*(speech) — Name Tongue — Taste Eye — Color Ear — Sound

<table>
<tr>
<td>
<ul>
<li>All these are food to death and death is food to God, whom should we pray</li>
<li>When a liberated person dies, do his organs depart</li>
<li>When an illuminated person dies, what that does not leaves him</li>
<li>What happens when an unilluminated person dies</li>
</ul>
Thereby Artabhaga held its peace
</td>
<td>
Mind Desire
Hand Work
Skin Touch
<ul>
<li>Fire is death of all being is food to water, which is death of death</li>
<li>No, they merged in Grahas and Atigrahas in form of impression merged in him</li>
<li>Name, it is infinite as viswdeva</li>
<li>“I cannot tell you in public”, took him away and said, by Karma or action one becomes good or bad accordingly</li>
</ul>
</td>
</tr>
<tr>
<td>
Bhujya

Where the decedents of Parikshit went after death (Emperor performed Ashwameda yagya or supreme horse sacrifice)

Thereby Bhujya held its peace
</td>
<td>
They are in the world of truth, which is thirty-two day’s journey of sun chariot and place is twice as earth and ocean twice as ours.

There is interspace between ours and that world like edge of razor, fire in the form of falcon delivers them to wind and wind placing them on itself led to that place, therefore wind is individuality
</td>
</tr>
</table>

<table>
<tr><td></td><td>or vyasti and totality or samasti is to be praised</td></tr>
<tr><td>Ushasta
• Explain me the brahman or supreme self, that is immediately and directly perceived
• Tell me precisely like this is cow and that is horse
Thereby Ushasta held its peace</td><td>• It is within us all, its breath through prana, moves down through apana pervades through vyana and goes out through udana
• You cannot see the seer, you cannot hear hearer, you cannot think of thinker, cannot know the knower and so the self is within us all</td></tr>
<tr><td>Gargi – I
• if all is pervaded in water, then where water is pervaded
• Where World of air is pervaded
• Where World of sky is pervaded
• Where the world of Gandhervas is pervaded
• Where World of sun is pervaded
• Where the World of moon is pervaded</td><td>• World of Air
• World of Sky
• World of Gandhervas (celestial musicians)
• World of Sun
• World of Moon
• World of Stars</td></tr>
</table>

• Where the World of star is pervaded • Where world of Gods is pervaded • Where world of *Indra* is pervaded • Where the world of *Viraj* is pervaded • Where the world of *Hiryangarbha* is pervaded Thereby *Gargi* held its peace	• World of Gods • World of *Indra* or king of Gods • World of *Viraj* or first creation • World of *Hirayangarbha* or first manifestation • Do not question too much, otherwise your head will fall, we should not ask too much of deities.
Aruna • *Sutra* or thread by which these world & other worlds are all held together • *Sutra or* thread by which inner controller and other world are controlled • *Sutra* or thread that inner controller, brahman or supreme self, world, Gods, *vedas* are all tied and knowns everything Thereby *Aruna* held its peace	• *Vayu* or air is the thread by which this world and other worlds are held together • It is yourself the immortal inner controller, it inhabitates earth, water, fire, sky, air, heaven, sun, quarters (direction), moon, darkness, light etc. yet it is within each of us. • It is yourself the inner controller and is immortal, rest everything is perishable

***Gargi* – II** she seeks permission for two questions	
• What pervades that *sutra* or thread, which is above heaven, below earth along with earth, heaven and space between it.	• *Akasha* or space/ether, the unmanifested universe during the phase of projection, continuation & dissolution
• What pervades *akasha* (*Gargi* tried to put *Yajanvalkya* in dilemma as question is not answerable since *akasha* pervades in brahman or supreme self which cannot be explained)	• Knower call brahman or supreme self as imperishable, it is neither gross nor subtle, neither long nor short, neither shadow nor dark, neither air nor *akasha* and cannot be perceived, non-effulgent, but indicate brahman or supreme self by denial of qualifying attributes, however with inferential evidence as orderliness of creation bhraman can also be inferred. Under his mighty rule sun and moon are held in respective position and so as the heaven, earth, time, day/night, seasons etc. are held at place, another evidence of imperishable is sacrifices, austerities performed without knowing him for thousands of years finds its perishable, this imperishable is never seen but

Thereby *Gargi* held its peace	is the seer, never heard but is hearer, never known but is knower. Bhrahman or supreme self, which is self is within all and beyond relative attributes by which unmanifested *akasha* or space/ether pervades, and it is the ultimate truth.
Vidaghdha • How many Gods are there	Mentioned in *Nivid* which is Group of mantras in *Rigveda* as *Vishwdeva* or universal God Thirty-three – Eight *vasus,* eleven *rudras,* twelve *adityas, Indra* and *Prajapati* *Vasus* – Fire, earth, air, sky, sun, heaven, moon and stars – in them all universe is placed *Rudras* – Ten organs (five sensory and five motor organ) of human body and mind – when they depart, people weep

• Which is the deity for the body, whose vision is intellect, light is mind and supports body and mind	*Adityas* – Twelve months of year – It carry all of them *Indra* – Thunderbolt or king of Gods *Prajapati* – sacrifices or creator Among them are six Gods (fire, earth, air, sky, sun and heaven) & three among these six are three world and two Gods among three- matter & Vital breath or *Prana*, one and half among two – air being one and half by its presence,by that everything attains glory and finally one God- *Hiryangarbha* or creator, which is brahman and also called *tyat* or something in remote.
o Earth	o Nectar– Essence of food
o Lust (*kama*)	o Women
o Color	o Truth (eye), sum product of eye of *viraj*
o Akasha	o Quarters (direction) – produced from ear of *viraj*
o Darkness	o Death
o Water	o *Varun* or rain
o Semen	o *Prajapati* or creator of the world

• Quarter or directions with their deities	
○ East	○ Sun, supported by eye which gets support from color and finds support at heart
○ South	○ *Yama* or God of justice, finds support at sacrifice gets support at renunciation which gets support at faith which is by support of heart
○ West	○ *Varun* or God of rain, finds support at water which find support at semen which find support at heart
○ North	○ *Soma* or moon, finds support at initiatory rites which find support at truth which find support at heart
○ Fixed direction (overhead)	○ Fire which supports in speech which finds support at heart
○ All find support at heart eventually, where heart finds support	○ Heart finds support in ourselves, otherwise one would be dead (self is said to be placed in heart)
• Where do body and heart find support	
○ Heart finds support	○ *Prana* (breath in)

o Where *Prana* finds Support o Where *apana* finds support o Where *Vyana* finds support o Where *udana* finds support Thereby *Vidaghdha* held its peace	o *Apana* (breath out) o *Vyana*(breath distributed in body) o *Udana* (all three held together) o *Samana*

Having defeated all *Yajanavalkya* further said "man is like a tree with leaves as hair and trunk as body, when tree is cut it grows again from root, if roots are destroyed then born again from seed, this happens to human also this is all by brahman"

Chapter 4

Once *Yajanvalkya* arrived at the place where king *Janak* was performing *Vajpeya vagya* (As ruler of country) and king enquired to him sarcastically for the purpose of his visit, if it is for gift of cattle's or hear discussion among scholars for which *Yajanvalkya* said both.

Yajanvalkya asked what your teachers have told you, for which king replied

King *Janak*	*Yajanvalkya*
o *Jitvan* told me that speech (fire) is brahman	o Anyone with good education will say that, how about muted person and where is its abode in body and how it gets

	support, otherwise your brahman is lame
○ No, please tell	○ Its abode is organ of speech and gets support from *akasha* (unmanifested universe) and that is to be meditated upon
○ *Udanka* told me that vital breath (*prana*) is brahman	○ Anyone with good education will say that, how about person who do not live (dead), otherwise your brahman is lame
○ No, please tell	○ Its abode is heart and support is akasha and that is to be meditated upon, through vital breath one performs all rituals
○ *Barku* told me that eye (sun) is brahman	○ Anyone with good education will say that, how about blind person and where is its abode in body and how it gets support, otherwise your brahman is lame
○ No, please tell	○ Eye is the abode of brahman, and support is *akasha* and that should be meditated upon
○ *Gardabhivipita* told me that ear is brahman	○ Anyone with good education will say that, how about deaf person and where is its abode in body and how it gets support, otherwise your brahman is lame

o No, please tell	o Ear is an abode and *akasha* as support and that is to be meditated upon, it is quarter (direction) one may go and never reaches its end are brahman
o *Satyakama* told me that mind is brahman o No, please tell	o Anyone with good education will say that, how about lunar person and where is its abode in body and how it gets support, otherwise your brahman is lame o Mind is abode and *akasha* is its support and that is to be meditated upon, for the sake of mind man desires
o *Vidaghdha* told me that heart is brahman o No, please tell	o Anyone with good education will say that, how about person without heart (dead) and where is its abode in body and how it gets support, otherwise your brahman is lame o Heart is an abode of brahman and *akasha* is its support and that is to be meditated upon

King *janak* arose from his lounge and approached *yajanvalkya* and offered salutation and seek instruction from him, he said as one procure chariot for long distance travel, the same way mind knows names of brahman, honored with wealth and studied *vedas / Upnishads*, now you must know where you will go after released from body.

Deity in right eye is *Indra* or king of Gods and left eye is *Viraj* or first manifestation, *akasha* or space/ether lies within the heart is the place of union of two, there food is blood vessel in heart or *Pinda* wrapped in net like structure in heart, it is by this path they move in body in sleep and waking state are called nerves or *hita* and subtle body in *Taijasa* or dream state receive food from gross body which is *Vaisvanara* or waking state. *Taijasa* atman which functions during dream state becomes *prajna* during dream less state.

Aspirant first realizes his identity or *aham* with *vaisvanara,* and next with *Taijasa* or dream state and then with *Prajna* or dreamless state and finally become one with *Turiya* or pure consciousness, this realized self is described as not this or not that and is imperishable, unattached and ever free.

Long back king *Janak* and *Yajanvalkya* had discussion during *Agnihotra* (daily ritual), where *Yajanvalkya* gave boon to king, which king wanted to exercise now by asking any question to him, king asked what serves light to man, *Yajanvalkya* answered, sun and when sun sets moon, when moon sets then fire, when fire sets then sound (one can go to a place in dark following sound), these all are external luminous object to illuminate external objects. When sound stops then self is the light (internal light to illuminate internal objects) and this is *purusa* or individual self, identified as intellect during waking state (*Vijnanamaya*) and is midst of organs. It wanders between two worlds (waking and dream state).

Person (individual soul) when born (assumes body) is joined with evil and when body dies, he discards evil (body and organs are means of engaging in activity good or bad, is from standpoint of supreme self). In dream he takes impressions of all embracing the world of waking state and makes the body unconscious and creates a dream body which is revealed by its own light and dreams, person is self-illuminated at this state.

Since there are none of physical accessories to him in dream state, he creates all objects from the modification of mind stimulated by his previous actions and becomes agent of creation, the effulgent being or *purusa* travels alone and makes body insensible in sleep, but he remains awake and taking with him luminous particles of object (impressions) and remains just an observer and dormant (impressions are devoid of physical form), the infinite being (*purusa*) travels alone and body is guarded by vital breath (*prana*) and he moves out and wander wherever he likes (it is popular belief that sleeping person should not be awakened suddenly, it may cause disorientation of organs of senses), it is pity that *atman* or individual soul is totally distinct from body and organs is self-evident but people do not notice that.

Entity (*purusa*) after enjoying and roaming in dream state and witnessing only good and evil reverts to its former condition and remains unaffected by whatever he observes in dream state (self being detached from body and organs are devoid of activity, thus it does not acquire merit or de-merit of dream experience). Even in waking state entity (*purusa*) is just witnessing good and evil and does not acquire fruit of action. It establishes the idea that self is light and distinct from body & organ and is not attached, it moves by turn from waking to dream state and vice versa.

Result of knowledge about individual self or *Atman* is to identity itself with all being and result of ignorance is self or *Atman* identity with finite things which are separate from each other, when things are separate, they can be killed, overpowered etc. hence ignorance represents infinite self as finite. Ignorance is not a natural characteristic of self or *Atman*, and it automatically reduces with knowledge, true form of self or *Atman* is free from desire, evil and fear.

Atman or individual self is directly perceived in the state of dreamless sleep which is free from ignorance, desire, duty, beyond all relations, all social and scriptural obligations and ephemeral objects, at this state on account of absence of duality, *Atman* or self does not see any object and is self-effulgent (factor causing vision in waking and dream state are mind, organ of perception and forms are all due to ignorance as something different from self), in deep sleep they are all unified and nothing to see when there is no second thing, in deep sleep it becomes transparent like water or crystal and witness one without second.

As heavily loaded cart moves along cracking, so the self-identified with body moves along groaning and breath becomes difficult (as death approaches) body grows thin becomes emaciated through old age or disease then like ripe mango or fig becomes detached to stalk, as so the infinite being detaching himself from body moves again the same way it has come to another body.

Body on becoming weak and unconscious, all organs gather around self or *Atman* and reaches to heart and all perceiving deities (eyes, ears etc) turn back from all sides to inward and like leech moving on the blade of grass reaches the end and takes another blade of grass by allowing itself towards it, so does the self by throwing off this body to new body, organs under control of past *karma* (impressions) become active in new body.

As goldsmith takes a small portion of gold to fashion a new and better form so as self, fashions a new body in better form which is suited as per manes, *gandharavas*, Gods, *viraj* or *hiryangarbha* with five elements as building blocks.

Supreme self or brahman is identified with mind, vital breath, organ of perception, five elements and qualities (*guna*) in accordance to these one acts or behaves and so it becomes (by doing good becomes good or otherwise), however self or *Atman* is identified with desire only, as it desires so is its resolutions and so as its deed and whatever is deed it reaps (attachment of transmigrating self or *Atman* along with work attained in subtle body as clings) after exhausting result of work it did in this life, it return to world again for fresh work and it is for the person with desire, for the person without desire, his organs do not depart along with self or *Atman* and being pure self it merges with brahman or supreme self and mortal man becomes immortal to attain brahman in this body itself.

Brahman or supreme self is to be realized through mind only, it is unknowable and constant and brahman or supreme self should be realized in this form only, seekers of brahman learning about supreme self should alone practice this wisdom and not to think too much of words to describe it, it is waste of effort, for this reason, people long ago did not want children, since sprit was there goal and desire of children is desire of wealth which is desire of company and it is all that desire which bound person.

CHANDOGYA - Keys of knowledge

Long ago lived *Shwetaketu*, his father *Uddalak* told him to find teacher for himself and at the age of twelve he found a teacher and by the age of twenty-four he completed studies of all *vedas* and returned home, arrogant, self-willed and stiff necked.

Father enquired *Shwetaketu* that if he has asked his teacher about what makes man hear and what is not heard before and think what is not thought before and know what is not known before, for which *Shwetaketu* denied and *Uddalka* said, by knowing a lump of clay we can know all things made up of clay or by knowing a piece of gold we know all the ornaments made out of it, it may differ by name and form but are same clay or gold.

Some put across thought that there was nothing in the beginning and all has come out of nothing which is not possible, I put other way that in beginning there was just being alone with no second, then he brooded to be many and thought of creation, to begin with he created light from light water was created and from water food was created, these three (light, water and food) created various kind of creatures those were egg-born, womb born and soil born, the divine being brooded again that that I should go in these three created Gods (light, water and food) and I will give them life but not name and form, so he went in three Gods and each of the three Gods then further divided in three and again those three further divided in three.

Redness, no matter where it is found, is light, whiteness no matter where it is found is water and darkness is always a food, no matter how strange things look is a combination of three.

Gods	**Grossest**	**Midway**	**Finest**
Food	Excrement	Flesh	Mind
Water	Excrement	Blood	Life

Light	Bone	Marrow	Speech

Gods (light, water and food), when three Gods enter in man each divides again in three.

Hence the mind comes from food, life from water and speech from light.

Shewatketu requested to explain again, my son know the nature of sleep, when man sleeps he is united with that supreme being or brahman which is himself, we think it is enough to say he sleeps alone yet he sleeps with himself as tethered bird after flying in every direction eventually settles down on its perch in same way mind wandering in every direction settles down on its life, or as bees create honey by gathering juices from different flowers and mixing all into common juice and identified as honey, so as various creatures who merges in that being in deep sleep or death and being again is the seed and all else is expression, self can be visualized as tree, if we strike on trunk of tree it oozes sap but tree lives or if leaves are plucked still tree lives but when life departs tree then entire tree withers and the body of bereft dies, but not to self since self is seed.

Uddalaka asked his son to pluck a banyan fruit which he did and asked him to break it down to seed and was then told to brake seed where he did not find anything, the great banyan tree has sprung up from the same seed so small that one cannot see, the being is the seed and all other are his expression, then again *Uddalaka* told his son to put lump of salt in glass of water and see tomorrow, next day he asked son for the lump of salt which he could not find as it was dissolved, he asked his son to taste water from top, middle and bottom of the glass by turn and it tasted same salt, though you may not find being in the world but he is there everywhere, so the being is the seed and rest all are his expression.

If a man is taken out from prosperous province and abandoned in forest blindfolded he will turn here and there and scream, if some good man takes off his bandage from eyes and tell them to go in that direction, he may reach home asking a few places, similarly man initiated by his master finds a way back to himself and remains in the body till *karma* is exhausted and join to supreme self after that.

Relatives gathered around a sick man and asking him if he remembers them, sick man will remember till he has speech, after that speech merges to mind which is life and life is light (refer table above) and light being manifestation of supreme being, hence the being is seed of all and rest are all his expression.

Progressive worship of brahman till supreme being – *Narada* requested sage *Sanat Kumar* for teaching him that he does not know, for which *Narada* said he has studied all *veda*, history or *purans*, traditions, grammar, rituals, mathematics, astrology, logic, economics etc. as these all are elementary knowledge, but I do not know self.

*Sanat Kuma*r said that all you know are name of the knowledge only, meditation in sequence of superiority is

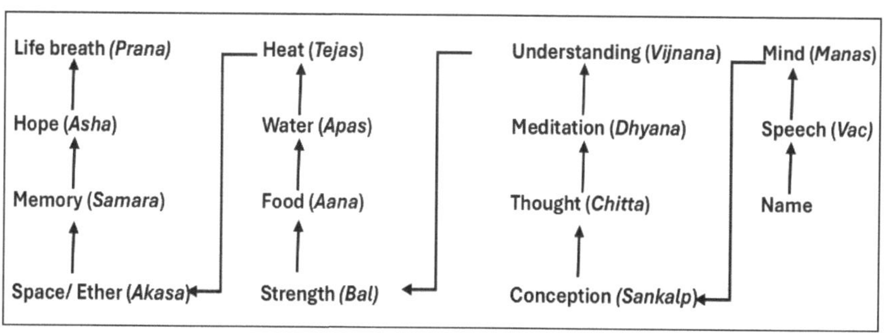

Superiority of meditation to be done upon the truth – *Narada* said what is the truth is to be found, as man cannot speak truth unless he knows it.

Sage *Sanat Kumar* said man who thinks, he knows and thinks about it, is only when one has faith on knowledge he has, and man gets faith by devotion only, act of devotion is done only when, man gets happiness and happiness is possible only when one has plenty of it, plenty or unlimited is when he sees nothing, hears nothing and knows nothing else and unlimited is immortal, unlimited depends on his own greatness, physical possession of things (cattle, gold etc.) are greatness to world for which one depends on another, whereas unlimited depends on nothing, he is self which is above, below, behind, front and everywhere. He who sees, thinks, knows this and love self, unite with self and for those who thinks otherwise are governed by others and are bound to lose what is gained and does not find pleasure eventually, he who thinks, feels and know this draw of life from himself, hopes from himself and everything from himself, pure food or thoughts creates pure intellect and pure intellect creates strong memory and strong memory cuts all knots of heart.

ISHA VASYA- The lord

Whatever there is, in this changing ephemeral world is enveloped by lord and by renunciation of the world, support yourself and do not covet wealth of anyone, as long as one is in human life and perform their assigned duties as ordained in scripture and live fullest for hundred years and *karma* will not cling to them.

Those whose life is demonic, blinded by the darkness or without knowledge returns to world again and again, self in one which is unmoving yet faster than mind, it is beyond reach of senses, ever steady but outstrip all the runs by its mere presence it enables all cosmic energies to sustain all activities in living being, it moves and does not moves at the same time, it is far and near as well, it is within us and outside to all of us.

Wise man perceives all being as not distinct from itself and itself as self as self of every being, by virtue of it he does not hate anyone, it is without taint of sin and radiant, it is everywhere without body, complete and pure, seeing all, encompassing all and assign duty to all including Gods and *Prajapati* or creator.

Those devoted to *avidya* or ignorance enters into blinding darkness and those who has entered into *vidya* have different results, both have to attain immortality through *vidya* or knowledge only, however through rituals one having conquered death through *avidya* or pure rituals, and at the same time worshiping unmanifested or *praktri / asambhuti*, enters blinding darkness and those devoted to manifested or *sambhuti* and *hiryangarbha* or first manifestation, enters into greater darkness. Result for both is different, he who understand *asambhuti* or unmanifested and *vinasha* or destruction, together enters immortality by devotion to *asambhuti* or unmanifested to conquers death by worship of *vinasha* or destruction and *hiryangarbha* or first manifestation.

Let my breath be merged with pervading *prana* or vital breath and body reduced to ashes, remembering good past deeds and pray – O fire, knowing all our deeds lead us by "fair path" for enjoyment of fruit of our *karma* and removal of crooked sins.

Fair path – path that soul takes after leaving body

- *Deva yana/ Arcirmarga* or path of Gods or path of light – eventually leads to the *satyaloka* or region of brahman, departs to different sphere sequentially from place of *agni* or fire in *suklapaksa* or bright half of lunar month to northern solstice to *devas* or deities to *vayu* or air to sun to moon to *varun* or water to *Indra* or king of Gods to *Prajapati* or creator and remains in *brahman loka or* abode of brahman till end of cycle (continuation till dissolution of universe) eventually absorption with brahman.
- *Pitra yana* or path of manes – departs to different sphere from fire to smoke in darkness to night to southern solstice to *pitraloka* or abode of ancestors to space/ ether and then to *chandraloka* or abode of moon to enjoy fruits of good *karma* till it is exhausted and reborn back to earth with residual *karma.*

KENAO – At whose command

Enquirer asked, "by whose command mind goes toward object and at whose direction vital forces and senses (eyes, ears, speech etc.) proceed to perform duties."

Replied that "he is ear of ear, mind of mind, speech of speech, life of life, eye of eye hence wise man giving up self-identification with senses and renouncing the world becomes immortal", brahman is different from what is known and beyond unknown (cannot be known by any means).

Brahman is not an object people worship but it is

- Not uttered by speech but by which speech is revealed
- Not comprehended by mind but mind is encompassed
- Not seen by eyes but by which man perceive activity of eyes
- Not heard by ears but by which man knows ears
- Not smelled with organs but by which organ of smell is impelled

If one thinks, I know brahman well enough then he know only a little expression of brahman it has on human body, and if one think he do not know brahman, even that is not enough, it is unknown equally to those who know brahman well, and to those who do not know, brahman is known through revelation only and it leads to freedom, one who finds brahman finds truth but if failed to find, sinks among fouler shapes and one who see same brahman in every creature and clings to none attains immortal life.

Once Gods were elated with victory, and was indeed of brahman only, knowing these pretensions of Gods, brahman appeared and all Gods could not make out.

They asked fire to find out, brahman enquired him its power, "I can burn all in earth", brahman placed a straw and fire with all its might could not burn.

Air went to him, brahman enquired him its power, "I can blow anything on earth", brahman placed a straw and air with all its might could not blow.

Indra or king of Gods went to him, as *Indra* approached him, he vanished and there appeared a pretty girl, the goddess of wisdom and *Indra* enquired about that mysterious person, she said it was brahman and to his victory you elated thus *Indra* learnt it was brahman, for this reason fire, air and *Indra* excel other Gods since they touched in proximity of brahman, it is instruction through analogy.

In lightning it is light to an eye, the light belongs to brahman, he should be worshiped as God by concentration, and cessation from sense objects. Rituals etc are leg of brahman, *vedas* are limbs and truth as its abode, knowing this and having dispelled sins, remains firm are seated in boundless bliss.

KATHO - Kathak branch of Veda

Once upon a time king *Vajasrava* desirous of fruit was giving away thing dear to him, *Nachiketa* his son was upset since gift he was giving away was only old cows, he asked his father to whom he wish to offer me and asked repeatedly, father annoyed by his pestering, told him in anger that "I give you to death".

Nachiketa sorrowfully cogitated in solitary place thinking my father must have spoken out of anger, but his utterance must not be falsified and went to abode of death. He waited for death at its place for three nights, upon return death said, "you waited for me for three nights without food or water, ask me three boons one for each night".

First boon – May my father be freed from anxiety and calm his mind thus freed from anger toward me and was granted by death.

Second boon – Teach me correct rituals of fire sacrifice, which is aid to gain heaven immediately. *Yama* or death described and taught ritual in elaborate way about kind of bricks and quantity that goes in alter and way to build that and told him "world comes out of this fire", *Nachiketa* understood clearly and repeated exactly as he was taught, death was delighted with his intellect and granted him an additional boon, this this ritual will be known as "*Nachiketa* fire" with splendid chain of many shapes, count of links of chain and worship triple fire (knowledge, meditation and practice) and triple process (evidence, inference and experience), triple duty (study, concentration and renunciation) and these all comes from brahman, it is brahman alone to be sought and found, when man understand himself, union of two kindle fire, a triple fire offers sacrifice and by this while being on earth breaks bound of death and mount into heaven.

Third boon- Some say when man dies, he continues to exist and others say that he does not, please explain.

Death was reluctant to explain and tried to allude *Nachiketa* with other material things, "it is deep and difficult to explain, choose something else", I offer you sons and grandsons, cattle's, horses, elephants, gold, great kingdom anything from this world that satisfy your desire, even take something beyond reach of human as fine women, their musical instruments, mount beyond dream but do not ask what lies beyond death (*Yama* was testing, if he is fit for knowledge).

Nachiketa said, these things are fleeting, joy ends at enjoyment, longest life is short, wealth cannot satisfy man, when I have choice of decaying life, I will not choose subject of death, I will not change my mind.

Having tested *Nachiketa* and found fit, death explains

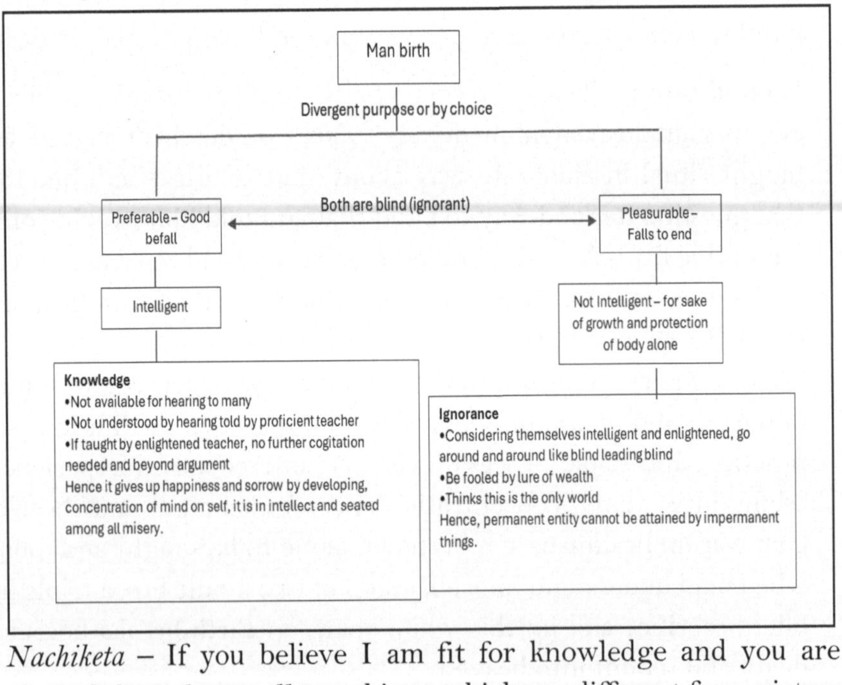

Nachiketa – If you believe I am fit for knowledge and you are pleased then please tell me, things which are different from virtue, different of vice, different from cause and effect and different from past and future.

Brahman	It is neither born nor die, it has not originated from anything and nothing originate from it and is not injured when body is killed
	It is lodged in heart of every creature, a desireless man sees glory of that self through serenity of organs
	While sitting, it travels far away and while sleeping it goes every where
	Meditate on self as bodyless midst body, permanent midst impermanent, great and pervasive
	Can not be known through study, intellect or by hearing, it can be known through self only. Aspirants pray them and self-reveals its true nature.

Death – All *vedas* in profound voice and all austerities speak of "OM" (Aum – as symbol of brahman) for *hiryangarbha* or first manifestation and supreme self as well, one desiring any of it, comes to him.

By the analogy of chariot, organ of senses as horse and intellect as charioteer with uncontrolled mind or bridle becomes devoid of

discrimination, and master of chariot or self, do not attain goal through intellect or charioteer, while Intellect associated with restrained mind and endowed with discrimination takes master to attain goal, which is place of *Vishnu* or principal lord.

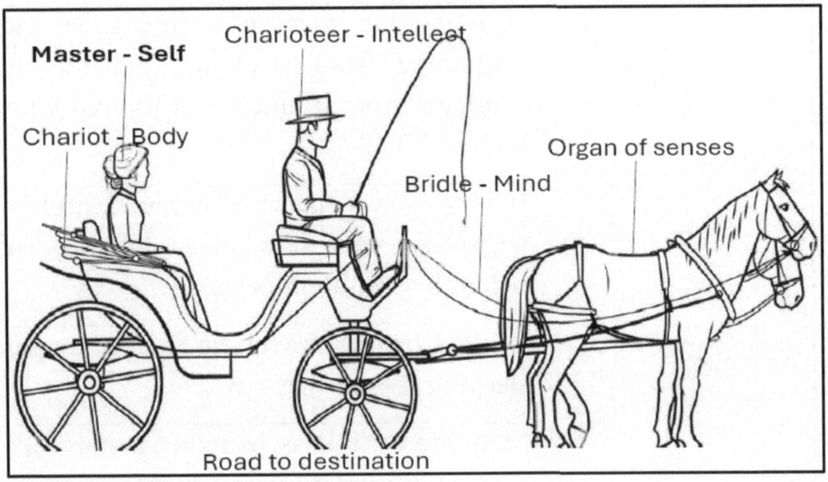

Hierarchy of objects

Means of attainment is, by merging organs of senses to mind, mind to intellect and intelligent self to great soul, hence arise, awake and learn by approaching learned one, since path is impassable as razor edge, self is hidden in all beings and is seen through pointed and fine intellect.

Purusa - Unmanifested (Highest goal, hidden in All being and to be seen through intellect) ➤ Unmanifested ➤ *Mahat* (*Hiryangarbha*) ➤ Soul ➤ Intellect ➤ Mind ➤ Sense object ➤ Sense

Obstacle to fine intellect are senses, since God created senses to turn outward hence it looks outward, daring ones looks back and finds himself. Ignorant man runs after pleasure and sinks into entanglement of death and by knowing the self who is eater of fruit of action and creates past and future does not fear anything. Tell your mind, there is but one who wonders from death to death, imagine it in your heart with size no bigger than thumb and knower of past and future which is burning like flame with no smoke, knowing him as rain upon mountain ridge from which water runs down the slope, man having seen this as self sees them everywhere.

Brahman is difficult to know, ascertaining in another way

One which is unborn and living in body is compared to a city with eleven gates (seven in head, three at lower including navel and one at top of head), meditate upon him as seen in the sky, fire in the altar, guest in house and air that goes everywhere. He breathes in and out, but when freed from body nothing remains, and no material then lives by breathing in and out, so it is self where breath finds its place.

Then *Yama* or God of death explains to *Nachiketa* secret of undying spirit and what happens after death, some souls enter womb for acquiring body and other as motionless object in accordance with their *karma* and deeds.

As fire assumes shape of its fuel, the self-inside all being assumes form with respect to each of its shape and yet it remains outside, another way to illustrate is, as air assumes distinct form with respect to different shape, similarly self-inside all being assumes different form and yet it is outside.

If single entity is self which is common to all then, sorrow of world should belong to brahman, however it is not so, as sun looking at entire world is not tainted by ocular and defect of world, in the same way self is not tainted by sorrow of world, and it is transcendental. Eternal peace is for those who are discriminating and realize in their heart as him being one and inner self of all and makes a single form multifarious.

Nachiketa asked, "where shall I find joy beyond all words, does it reflect light or glow by itself".

Death said – Nothing illuminates him, but when it shines everything begins to shine.

All this universe emerges and moves due to supreme brahman, which is scary like thunderbolt and one who knows this become immortal, from his fear fire burns, sun shines, *Indra*/ air/ death runs, as one sees himself clearly in mirror so as with intellect as mirror sees brahman, having understood this and discriminates senses and their rising and settling and do not grief.

Brahman is incomprehensible and self is reveled through deliberation of intellect or ruler of mind, when five senses come to heart and rest along with mind and intellect is the highest state and keeping the sense sturdy as in *yoga.*

Nachiketa – If it cannot be attained through speech, mind, eye etc, then how to ensure its existence.

Death – Go backward from effect to cause until you are compelled to believe him and truth will be drawn, and mortal becomes immortal when

- Desire in the heart is finished
- The knot of heart is cut
- Heart has hundred and one arteries and one of those is *sushumna,* which runs till head, one who climbs through it attains immortal, otherwise drive in vortex.

God the innermost self, which is no bigger than thumb lives in heart, man should strip him of the body as arrow maker strips the reed.

TAITTIRYA – Taittirya branch of Veda

May friends, *Varun* or Water, *Indra or* King of Gods, *Birhaspati* or teacher of Gods, *Vishnu* or one of principle deity of long stride be blissful to us and *Vayu* or air being immediate brahman protect me and my teacher *OM shanti* (peace), *Om shanti* (Peace), *Om shanti* (peace).

Meditation on juxtaposition

- Related to world – Earth and heaven, with *vayu* or air as link between two and sky being rallying point
- Related to shining things – Fire and sun, with lightning as link between two and water being rallying point
- Related to knowledge – Teacher and student, with instruction as link between two and knowledge being rallying point
- Related to progeny – Mother and father, with generation as link between two and progeny as focal point
- Related to body – lower jaw and upper jaw, with tongue as link between two and speech being rallying point

Pray to God to fill me with intelligence that I may grasp immortality and make my body strong, tongue sweet, ears keen and keep me away from forgetting with spiritual riches, I shall never lack cloths, food, drinks to serve you better.

Bhuh, Bhuvah, Suvah are sacred sound and fourth being *Mahas* which is spirit (God) and other these are limbs.

- When *Bhuh* is earth, *Bhuvah* is sky, *Suvah* is heaven then *Mahas* is sun since everything is sustained by sun
- When *Bhuh* is fire, *Bhuvah* is wind, *Suvah* is sun then *Mahas* is moon as all planets are sustained by moon

- When *Bhuh* is *Rigveda*, *Bhuvah* is *Samveda*, *Suvah* is *Yajurveda* then *Mahas* is brahman as all is sustained by brahman
- When *Bhuh* is *prana*, *Bhuvah* is *apana*, *Suvah* is *wyana* them *Mahas* is food since living is sustained by food

Hence four times of each of above four makes sixteen sound, he who knows are knower of brahman and *Mahas* is brahman as *OM* also.

God lives in hollow of heart and things that hangs down between palates like teat is the path of brahman reaching till head where the hair parts (customary) and it passes by separating skull and established in fire or *Bhuh*, air or *Bhuvah*, sun or *Suvah* in brahman which is *Mahas* and becomes lord of mind, ruler of speech, ruler of eye, ears and knowledge, overall he becomes brahman embodied in *akasa* or space/ether.

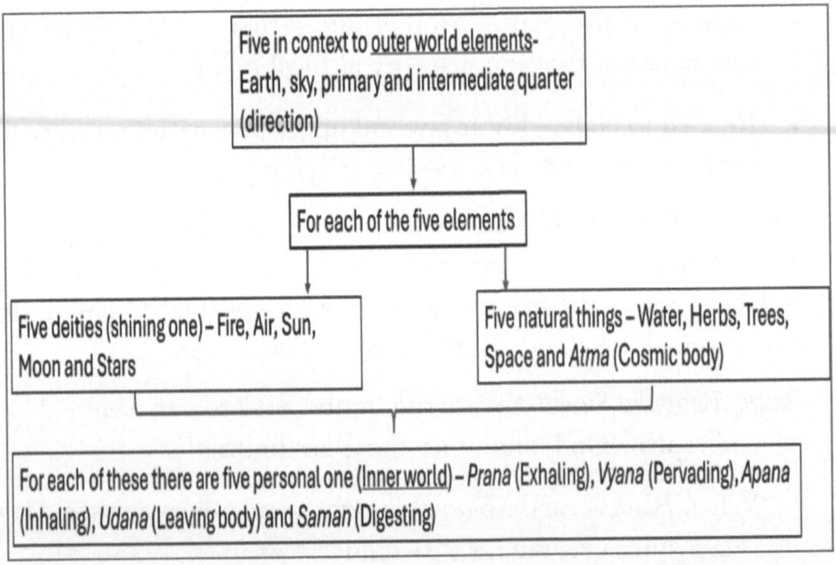

Imagining all these Constituent by five Factors, one fills up outer five-fold with inner fivefold. Meditation on brahman as identified with "*Vyahritis*" or speech and followed by, conceived as fivefold entity to be enjoined as meditation on "*OM*", though *OM* is mere word, it becomes means of attaining brahman or *hiryangarbha* or first manifestation in accordance with meditation done upon. *OM* is brahman, *OM* permits and begins the ceremony, all chants begin with *OM*, all hymns begin with *OM*, his command is in the name of *OM*, teacher begin with *OM* and pupil begin with *OM*.

Duty is considered as contributory to attainment of human goals, learn and teach truth, austerity, control outer and inner organ, kindle and keep fire, *agnihotra* (daily ritual), good social conduct, progeny and procreation.

Mantra for self-recital for the sake of development of knowledge and purification of mind

"oṃ ahaṃ vṛkṣasya reriva ǀ kīrtiḥ pṛṣṭhaṃ gireriva, ūrdhvapavitro vājinīva svamṛtamasmi, draviṇaṃ savarcasam, sumedhā amṛtokṣitaḥ, iti triśaṅkorvedānuvacanam, oṃ śānti: śānti: śānti"

"I am the seed (originator) of the tree (world), my glory rises like the peak of the mountain, high and pure as the sun, I am verily immortal, my wealth is the effulgence of brahman, I am the immutable and immortal brilliance, this is the message of wisdom from Sage Trisanku, oṃ santi, santi, santi

Instruction to student after imparting knowledge of *veda*

Speak truth, practice righteous, make no mistake in studies, offer desirable wealth to teacher, do not cut line of progeny, no mistake in protecting yourself, not to be careless in learning and teaching.

No error in duties toward God and manes, let mother be goddesses and father, teacher, guest be your God. Do not work which is blameworthy, offer seat and hospitality to praiseworthy, offering should be make with honour, with modesty and awe in friendly way. If in doubt on duty and custom then behave in matter as praiseworthy will do, if they would have been at your place.

Joy

Brahman is truth, knowledge and infinite, it exists in intellect and lodged at space in heart, where sequence of creation of "elemental man" or created out of five elements eventually merges to food

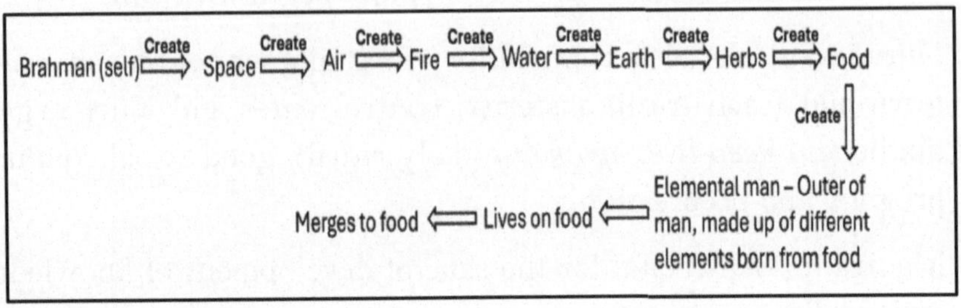

Joy of the elemental man

Foundation	**Left arm**	**Right arm**	**Head**	**Heart**
Earth	*Apana* (Exhaling)	*Vyana* (distribution of air)	*Prana* (Inhaling)	Self-air
Sage– *Atharwangiras*	*Sanmantra* – Prayer	*Rig matra* – Rituals	*Yajur matras* – Prayer	*Veda*
Mahat – discrimination	Truth	Righteous	Faith	Concentration
Brahman	**Hilarity – contentment**	**Pleasure**	**Joy – Satisfied desire**	**Bliss**

Elemental man is imagined, with different parts and their outcome at heart.

Worship each to acquire results accordingly.

- Worship food as brahman and acquire all food
- Worship vital forces as brahman and attain full span of life
- Worship on faith and attain discrimination with body and self
- Knowledge actualizes at sacrifice (duties in *veda*) and execute duties

If anyone feels brahman is nonexistent then he himself becomes nonexistent, since all are his creation, and he is inside all his creation and brahman being ever blissful.

God thought to be many and to procreate, so in the heart of meditation he created everything and entered in everything and became form and formless, defined and undefined, sustaining and non-sustaining, sentient and insentient, true and untrue.

In beginning all was unmanifested or Brahman alone, from their it manifested itself hence it is self-created, self-creation is the source of joy and are fearless, whenever it has slightest difference with self, one is smitten with fear and that very brahman becomes terror to so called learned man who lacks unitive outlook.

Evaluation of bliss

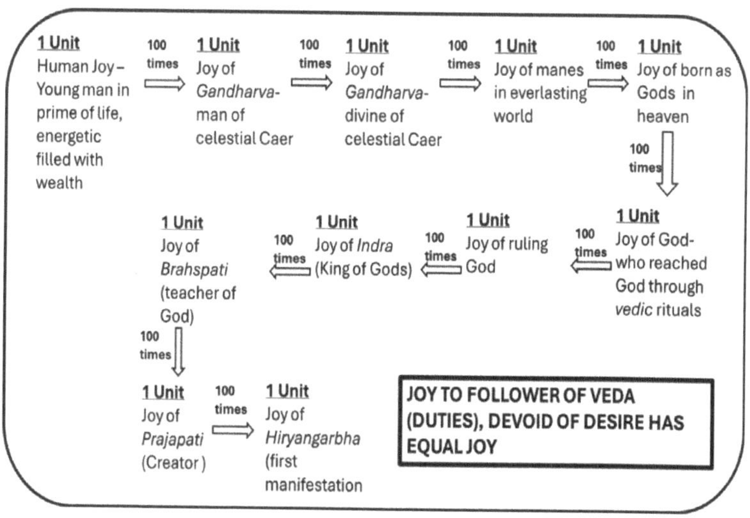

He who lives in man and sun as well, are same and by knowing this truth one goes beyond elemental self and attains self as made of vital forces to attain self-made up of bliss.

Enlightened man is not afraid of anything after realizing brahman which is synonyms to bliss and do not remorse for anything good or bad deeds.

Bhirgu

Bhirgu asked his father *Varun*, what is brahman

Varun – First meditate on food, life, seeing, hearing, speaking and then on brahman from whom all things are born, lives and move toward him and eventually returns to him.

Bhirgu meditated on food to understand that all things are born, lived and move toward food and eventually merged in food, with further meditation he found that all things are mind from which all things are born, lived, move toward and eventually merged to mind, he meditated again to find that knowledge is brahman from which all things are born, lived, move toward and eventually merges to knowledge, finally he meditated to find joy is brahman from which all things are born, lived, move toward and eventually merges to joy.

This is what *Bhirgu* son of *Varun* found out in the hollow of heart, he who knows this stands on rock and command everything, finds a family, gather flocks and heard grow famous through light of spirit and becomes great man

- Respect food since life is food, body lives on food and body are life and life is body, they are food to one another
- Do not steal food since water is food, light lives on water, water is light, and light is water they are food to one another
- Store food since earth is food, air lives on earth, earth is air, and air is earth, and they are food to one another

Never turn anyone from door and gather enough food, he who gives with purity gets purity in return, he who gives with passion gets passion in return and he who gives with ignorance gets ignorance in return, he who understand this and meditate upon brahman as blessing of all activity as speech, *prana* or inhalation & *apana* or exhalation, activity of hand, feet and even evacuation of bowel, hence bow down to brahman as sole object of desire and be the goal of all desire, worship brahman as master of all and become master of all.

He who knows this says goodbye to the world and goes beyond elemental self and living in self, thinking of self, knowing to self and joyous self.

MUNDAKA– In the feet of monk

Sunaka approached *Angiras* (from the linage of teaching from brahma- creator) and asked, what by knowing one thing all is known, he replied that there are two kinds of knowledge

- Lower – all *vedas,* science of pronunciation, codes of rituals, grammar, etymology, astrology etc
- Higher – knowledge of imperishable which cannot be perceived and grasped with mind, it is without source and does not possess any features (like eye, ears etc.), it is multiforme, all pervasive, extremely subtle, undiminishing and source of all.

As spiders spread its thread the same way earth grows its herbs, as humans grow its hair in the same way universe emerges, and sequence of creation is

Brahman ⇨ Food ⇨ *Prana (Hiryangarbha)* ⇨ Mind – cosmic intelligence ⇨ Five elements ⇨ World ⇨ *Karma*

Fruits of *karma* are acquired by yourself by virtue of duties performed with desire, it results in *karma* being accumulated, fruits of *karma* are perishable which depletes with enjoyment, ignorant people get elated with idea that it is bliss and undergo cycle of death and rebirth. Men engaged in *karma* under influence of attachment is affected to sorrow and deprived of heaven on exhaustion of fruits of *karma.* One detached to world have competency to higher knowledge and should go to master with versed in *veda* and absorbed in brahman, he should approach teacher with calm heart and controlled organs.

Imperishable called *purusha* or individual self and by knowing him all become known is the subject of higher knowledge, as thousands of sparks fly off from fully ablaze fire, similarly imperishable originates thousands of creatures and merges again into them.

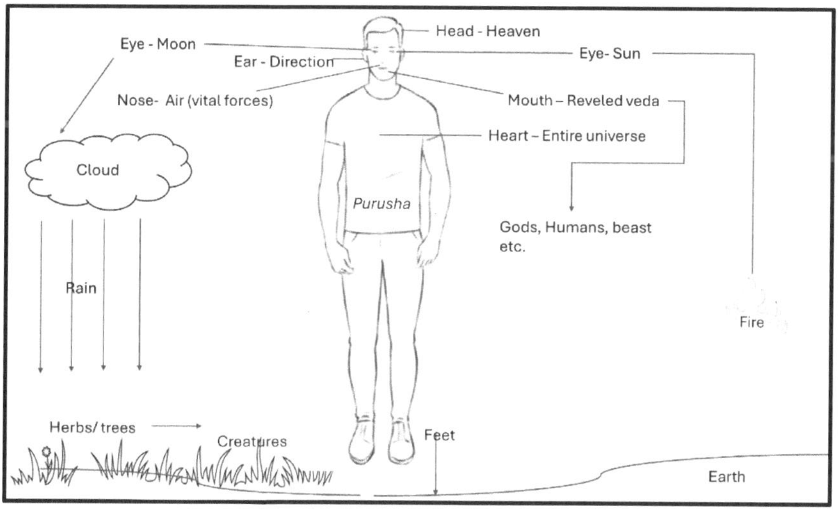

Purusha or individual self is transcendental since it is formless, coextensive with internal and external being. It is birthless with vital forces or *prana* and without mind, pure and superior to imperishable *maya* or illusion but from him all vital forces and mind originate, also from him senses, space, air, fire, water and earth that support everything originates.

It can be illustrated as heaven being head, moon and sun being eyes, direction being ears, reveled *veda* as speech, air is vital force or *prana* and entire universe as heart and from its feet earth originates. Fire originates from sun, clouds emerge from moon, herbs on earth originate from cloud and from there creatures emerges. All *vedas* emerges from *purusha* or individual self from that emerges Gods of various groups, *sadhyas* or achievers, human, beast, birds, life, vegetation, austerities, faith, truth, continence and dutifulness.

From *purusha* emerges

- Seven sense organs – all in head, two ears, two eyes, two nose and tongue
- Seven flames -blue or will of God, yellow or illumination, pink or cosmic love, white or purification, emerald green or healing

and manifestation, ruby gold or resurrection, violet or transmutation

- Seven kinds of fuel and their seven-fold objects, it by these objects the *prana* or vital breath and organ of senses are fed
- Seven-fold oblation by perception of seven fold objects at seven lakh seats of senses where *prana* or individual soul moves

Seven in seven of every living thing means omniscient *purusha* or individual self emerges, at all the *karmas* and fruit of *karma* to both with knowledge and ignorant one, all ocean, mountain, rivers and various vegetation emerges from him by the virtue of internal self that exist in midst of elements.

Purusha or individual self alone is all, with *karma* and knowledge being supreme, by knowing that immortal brahman existing in heart destroys knot of ignorance.

To know immutable, it being formless

It is effulgent and moving in heart and that is the goal, it is fixed in all sentient and insentient being, it is gross and subtle beyond ordinary knowledge of creatures and is most desirable, it is vital force, speech and mind this entity is true, immortal and to be pretended so shoot for it.

Hold the bow fix arrow on it, which is sharpened with meditation, draw string with mind absorbed in its thought and hit the target, which is imperishable, imagine OM as bow, soul as arrow and brahman as target and become one with it, as arrow hitting the target becomes part of target.

Imperishable is hard to grasp, it is presented repeatedly to make it comprehensible, self alone is like heaven, earth and space in between strung, give up all other talks and direct your mind, vital forces along with all organs as bridge leading to immortality.

As nerves are connected to heart and the same way spokes connected to wheel becomes multiforme, so move this with meditation on OM and free yourself from hindrances in going to other side of shore beyond darkness. Self is omniscient in general, knowing all in detail with such glory of self, seated at space in luminous city of brahman.

Condition your mind that, imperishable as carrier of vital forces and body and seated in cavity of heart, through this knowledge of discrimination, people realize the self as existing in its fulness everywhere, when self is realized which is both low and high then heart is united with him and all doubts solved and one's all action (*karma*) is dissipated.

To sum up, it is brahman in supreme bright sheath free from taint and is without parts, pure and light of all light, its place is where sun, moon or stars do not shine, it by his light everything else shine, it alone is true and everything else is its modification that exist.

Attaining higher knowledge – by knowing *purusa* as imperishable truth, that leads to total eradication of cause of worldly state (knots of heart) and *yoga* is means of realization.

Two similar bird (symbol of two aspect of same reality) clings on same tree, one eating fruit of divergent taste (*Jivatman* – individual soul enjoying fruit of *karma)* and other looks on without eating (*parmantman/ brahman* – neither attached nor repelled to object), it is metaphorically stated that one of them (eating fruit) is *jiva* or individual soul sunk in ignorance and grieves over his powerlessness being in deluded condition, but seeing the worshipfulness of other bird he takes him to the lord processioning all glory and majesty thus reveled of his dejection.

Seeking bird (one in trouble) behold golden-hued bird (enlightened bird) as the doer, ruler and the supreme being, at the very source of birth of universe and then became wise, it shakes off all deeds of merit and demerit and became taintless (pure) and attained supreme state of equanimity. It is the quality of brahman that lives in all being, by knowing him wise men has no desire and then engaged in act that brings inner delight, he who knows brahman as being is best among all men. Bright and pure self within the body with effort of attenuated blemishes sees it attainable through truth.

Truth alone wins, by truth the path of *devayana* (north road to sun, situated north of *nagavithi* or milky way and south of *saptrishi* or constellation ursa major where *siddhas* or perfected masters lives and have no rebirth) is laid by desireless seers ascend to place with supreme treasure and its attributes are, effulgent and unthinkable, it is subtler then subtle, shines diversely, it is farther then far off and close as on own hand among sentient being it is seated in the cavity of heart.

Means of realization are that, it cannot be comprehended by eyes, speech or by other senses nor through austerity or *karma*, however after becoming purified in mind, through intellect one can see indivisible self through meditation, one who attains own self wins those world which he mentally wishes for and those enjoyable things which he covets, hence one desirous of prosperity should adore to knower of self.

He who knows brahman as abode in which universe is placed and by which all shines, wise one after becoming desireless worship him and transcend this human seed, by eschewing desire is chief discipline for liberation, he who covets desirable things is born among those surroundings along with their desire, but for one whose all wishes are fulfilled and self-poised have all longing vanished even here.

Self is not attained through study nor through intellect or by hearing it, while self is attainable through seeking and it revels its own nature, self is not attained by one devoid of strength (vigor and constant adherence to self) or through delusion nor with knowledge unassociated with monasticism, one who strives through this means enters into the abode of brahman.

One entering into brahman – having attained brahman, seers is contended with knowledge, established in self which is free from attachment and is composed, by realizing its pervasiveness and discrimination of self and is merged in contemplation and enters in all, ascertained with *vedantic* knowledge and having become pure in mind through *yoga* of monasticism, then at the moment of departure becomes identified with supreme immortality in the world of brahman and free from all sides, as river flowing down becomes indistinguishable on reaching sea by giving up their name and form, so the illuminated soul having freed from name and form reaches effulgent *purusa* or supreme self which is higher than *maya* or illusion.Anyone who knows brahman becomes brahman indeed, he overcomes grief, rises above aberrations and freed from the knots of heart and attain immortality.

Rule of transmission of knowledge of brahman – it should be expounded to one engaged in practice of discipline, versed in *veda* and devoted to brahman and personally sacrifices to the fire called *Ekarsi* with faith and duly accomplished the vow of holding fire on head.

PRASHNA – Questions, elaboration of Mundka upnishad

Six people devoted to brahman approached teacher "*Pippalada*" in search to know highest brahman with dry branches of tree or fuel presented to teacher (token, presented to teacher whose direction is desirable), to them teacher said, "dwell with me for one year with austerity or *Tapas*, chastity or *Brahmcharya* and faith or *Shraddha*, then ask question you have and I will answer, one year later they return to ask their question.

"Kabandhin Katyayana" asked – from where creatures are born

Teacher said, *Prajapati* the creator, desirous of progeny performed austerity and created moon and sun and said to himself that these two should produce creatures for me in manifold ways, sun or *prana* is life and moon or *rayi* is food, everything in form or formless is food with sun and moon as pair.Sun when it rises enters eastern quarter or direction and thereby enfold living being of east with rays and then spread rays in all directions this enfold all living being, sun is soul of all creatures as described in *rik* or *Rigveda*.

Year have two path, southern and northern, to southern path are those who perform sacrifices or duties and are of pious action wins world of moon and return to earth again, this path is of manes or *rayi* or food, northern path are those who seek self through austerity, chastity, faith and knowledge and travels through northern path of sun, they are immortal, fearless and are final goal that is not to return on earth, this path is blocked for ignorant.

Some says sun are with five feet which are five season (summer, rain, autumn, fall+ winter and spring) and twelve fire or month of year, it dwells in the region above sky, other says world is fixed in omniscient sun endowed with seven wheels or seven color of light and six spokes or six season, but entire universe rests in *Prajapati* or creator who manifest as year and further evolves as months, moon or food/ *rayi* and sun or *prana*/ eater are component of month as they are from year. It is characterized by dark and bright fortnight of moon, though sun or *prana* is associated with bright fortnight, yet with wisdom as *prana* pervades in entire month, they see everything to be bright, hence even sacrifices performed in dark fortnight reaps fruit of bright fortnight, however one with ignorance do not see sun or *prana* in everything, do not reap fruit even one performed in bright fortnight.

One who follows rules of *Prajapati* or creator and observes austerity, chastity and truth is firmly established and belongs to *brahmloka* or abode of creator.

***"Bhargava Vaidarbhi"* asked** – how many Gods support body, how many of them manifest their power through him and among them who is paramount.

Teacher said, space/ ether (*akasha*), wind, fire, water, earth, speech, mind, eye and ears are Gods that manifest its glory and support and upholds this body, and among them *prana* or vital breath is chief most, it divides into five parts to support body and upholds it. As *paran* rise upward all other rise upward and when it settles down, they all settle down with it, as bees goes where queen bees go, *prana* burns as fire and it is sun, it is rain and *Indra* or king of Gods, it is wind, earth and food, it is luminous God, it is being and not being as well and immortal, as spokes are fixed to hub, in same way all are fixed to *prana* or vital breath.

Prajapati or creator moves in womb and it is he who is born and *prana* or vital breath is same as *Prajapati*, lord of creation who pervades in all, *prana* is carrier of oblation to God (fire is called carrier), it is first offering to manes and activity of *rishis*, it is *rudra* or destroyer, protector or *Vishnu*, it move in sky as sun, *prana* is rain which is source of food to all, all that exist here is under control of *prana* and also for that exist in heaven.

***"Kausalya Asvalayana"* asked** – when life is born, how does it come to body, how it distributes itself, establish itself and how does it depart from body, in what way it supports external and self.

Prana or vital breath is born of *atman* or individual soul, as shadow is cast by person, so is the *prana* by *atman*, it comes to body through the activity of mind and it distributes in body like emperor command others to take their respective places, so this *prana* employes others to it move to their respective place, hence sense organs are modification of chief *prana*.

Prana or vital breath engages *apana* in organ of excretion and generation, moves through mouth, nose and dwells in eyes and ears, middle of it is *samana* or modification of *prana* as food, from this *prana* arises seven flames (two eyes, two ears, two nostrils, and organ of speech), *vyana* or modification of *prana*, dwells in heart, where there are hundred and one arteries or *nadi* and each one of it has hundred branches and from each branch there are seventy two thousand subsidiary vessels and *vyana* moves in these, *Atman* or self, departs body through *udana* or modification of prana which moves from head to toe, ascending upward through conduit called *sushamna*, it departs to virtuous world for its virtuous deeds or to the sinful world for its sinful deeds.

External counterpart that controls internal	
Internal	**External controlling**
Prana – Inward, inspiring energy	Sun
Apana–Downward, eliminating energy	Earth
Udana – Upward, creative energy	Fire
Samana – Inward churning energy	Space between sun & earth
Vyana – Pervasive, circulating energy	Air

Reference to *atman* or self, *prana* or vital breath has its external counterpart where *prana* and its modifications in physical body have their cosmic counterparts and physical are controlled by cosmic counterparts.

Sun is external counterpart of *prana*, it rises favoring *prana* in ego or self-consciousness, while deity on earth controls *apana* and *akasa* or space between heaven and earth is *samana*, while air is *vyana* and fire is *udana* , one whose fire is extinguished goes out of rebirth with senses absorbed in mind and thoughts at the time of death along with the desires are absorbed in *prana* and *prana* are joined with fire, together with prana (along with desires) and soul leads to whatever world fashioned by thoughts.

***"Suryayanin Gargya"* asked** – What are that sleeps in man, and what remains awake in him, which deity that sees dream and who are at happiness in deep sleep, and to whom again all these gathers.

As rays of sun when sets are gathered in its luminous orb and again go forth when arise, so as object and senses become one in mind as mind is termed as superior God, at that time he does not perceive with senses, but *prana* or vital breath remains awake in body. It is at mind along with senses gathered into it, experiences the dream and not *atman* or inner self, hence dream is characteristic of mind not of self.

When *jiva* or embodied soul, conditioned with *upadhi* of mind is overcome by light or brahman he sees no dream, at this time body arises with happiness, in deep sleep body and senses does not functioning under influence of *avidya* or ignorance and desire remains actionless. *Atman* or individual self during waking and dreaming which appears in different form and is associated with *upadhis* or title of body and mind, but it manifest peace, non-duality and bliss in deep sleep which is true nature of self, in this state all gross and subtle elements are absorbed in *atman* or individual self, one who sees, feels, hear, smells, taste, thinks and know is doer but the intelligent self is *purusha* or supreme self is established in *atman* or individual self.

"Saibya Satyakama" **asked** – if someone meditate on *AUM* till death, which world does it wins

AUM is both higher (*parabrahman*) and lower (*aparbrahman*), one can attain eighter by meditating on it. If meditated on letter A (soul of *Rigveda)* then he is enlightened by that alone and comes back to earth, if meditated upon second letter U (symbol of *Yajurveda*) he attains intermediate space on plane of moon and having enjoyed fruits of good deed there returns back to earth (compared to dream state of sleep), meditating on *AUM* as symbol of *sagun brahman* or with qualities he is united with effulgent self as snake freed from skin and freed from all sin.

- A – waking state/ earth/ *Rigveda* which is *Virat (Deva-* God)
- U – Dream state/ Intermediate space between earth & heaven/ *Yajurveda* which is *hiryangarbha* or first manifestation
- M – Deep sleep/ Heaven/ *Samveda* which is *Ishrava deva* (divine)
- *AUM* – Brahman and liberation

Three letters of *AUM* if employed separately are mortal but when joined together and used properly on activity of external, internal and intermediate state (refer to state of waking, dreaming and deep sleep) realizes oneness with *sagun brahman* and overcome death and rebirth.

"Sukesran Bharadvaja" **asked** – who is the person with sixteen parts

Creation of parts is for purpose of reveling *purusha* or supreme self, who is otherwise part less, formless it is departure of whom we say, "I depart and by staying I stay".Sixteen entities described are sixteen parts belonging to *purusha* or supreme self.

He created *prana* or vital breath, then created faith and then created space in which rests air, fire, water, earth, organs, mind and food from which comes virility, austerity, *vedic* hymns, sacrifice and world of manes.

Sixteen parts are created through *avidya* or ignorance and are unreal like objects in dream. When *avidya* is destroyed they merge in *purusha* or supreme self, where names and form are like flowing river which is bound to ocean, and it disappears on reaching there and all are called ocean alone. *Purusha* or supreme self alone is to be known and all parts rest firm in him like spoke nave of wheel and there is nothing higher than this.

MANDUKYA – Master Mandukya

All that is past, present and future (manifested) is *AUM* and all those beyond threefold or unmanifested is also *AUM.*

AUM is symbol of both brahman or supreme self and *atman* or individual self and its points non-duality of *atman* and brahman. *Atman* can be perceived directly and immediately whereas brahman can only be inferred by it, as brahman is formless and beyond any perception.

Atman has four quarters or *padas*

Experiencer of external object	
Seven limbs	**Nineteen mouths**
• Head- Hevan • Eyes – Sun • Breath – Air • Heart – Fire • Middle part of body- *akasha*	• Five organs of perception -Hearing, touch, sight, taste and smell • Five organ of action – Speech, grasping, locomotion, generation and execration • Five *pranas* (Vital breath)- *Prana, apana, vyana, samana and udana*

• Belly- Water • Feet- Earth	• Mind (*manas*) • Intellect (*buddhi*) • Consciousness (*ahamkara/* ego) • Mind stuff (*chitta*)

1. **Waking state or *Jagrat/ Vaisvanara* of *atman* or individual soul – "A"**

Atman is conscious of external objects other than itself, and these outer objects has seven limbs which are parts of body, nineteen mouths, five *pranas* and three experiencer of gross objects which are superimposed on *atman* due to ignorance *or avidya.*

2. **Dreaming state or *Swapan/ Taijasa* of *atman or* individual soul – *"U"***

Atman is conscious of internal objects and experiencer is subtle body, these are impressions left by waking experiences which are perceived in dream as real as waking state, dreams are due to influence of ignorance, desire and action.

3. **Deep sleep or *Susupti / Prajana (without dream)* of *atman* or individual soul – *"M"***

All experiences of *atman* are unified, and it is at consciousness, full of bliss and is at the door leading to knowledge. In deep sleep no specific knowledge is present as in dark night all cows appear black and cannot be distinguished from one another, so as in deep sleep all discriminative knowledge disappears and friction caused by subject and object is absent and no effort is needed for anything, and one is at bliss.

All three states superimposed on atman is through ignorance or *avidya* and causal law (cause and effect) operates, however in fourth state of" *Turiya*" is the nature of pure consciousness and is the supreme reality and can be reached by negation of earlier three states.

4. Pure consciousness or *Turiya* of *atman* or individual soul – *"AUM"*

State at which, *atman* is not conscious of inner or subjective world nor of outer or objective world, neither both of the world, at the same time is not unconscious also, at this state all is at peace, all bliss and everything non- dual. This state cannot be perceived, cannot be related to anything or comprehended, described but can be experienced only.

Refutation of erroneous superimposition can be grasped by one endowed with sharp and moderate intelligence but for majority of people, they can concentrate on *'AUM"* as symbol of reality.

"AUM TAT SAT" - *AUM* is truth

BHRAMSUTRA

Nyaya prasthana – Yukti (reasoning)

Commentary by "*Adi Sri Shankracharyya*"

Bhramsutra also known as *vedant sutra* is attributed to *Badarayana*, also called *Vyasa*, it is the compilation of five hundred and fifty five verses or *sutras* in this text, it criticizes metaphysical dualism by refutation of all competing arguments on dualism, and brings harmony among various *upnishads*, which were written by different sects at different point of time and have contradictory assertions, if not understood properly.

It postulates that, brahman is the supreme God which is only source of origin of everything and is the material cause (material required for creation) and the efficient cause (skill and accessories required for creation), including individual soul or *atman* in each one of us.

Chapter 1 – Valid means of Knowledge

Chapter 2 – Contradictions

chapter 3 – Transmigration

chapter 4 - Result

Chapter 1 - *Samanvaya* "Reconciliation through correct interpretation"

Section I

Thereafter (studies of *vedas* and duties) deliberation on Brahman is to be undertaken.

Brahman being without definition and cannot be deliberated upon, however entire universe is derivative of him hence Brahman must be omniscient and the source of primordial scriptures or *vedas* and these scriptures must be a only source of valid means of knowledge, once Brahman is fully understood through *upnishad* it culminates in knowledge with no connection to action.

Upnishad mentions that Insentient being or *Preadhana*, is not the cause of universe

Objection	**Refutation**
Upnishad mentions "self", then seeing others become secondary sense.	Liberation is promised to one who holds on "self" (sentient one) and does rejects self as insentient, eventually merger of all in self which is not possible for insentient one merging to sentient.

Upnishad revels that supreme consciousness is the cause of all manifestation, and this self is blissful and repeated several times in scripture.

Objection	**Refutation**
Brahman is not blissful since word denoting is modification of word (Suffix added to "*Anandamaya*", *Anand*- bliss & *Mayat* – made of) word *Mayat* in Sanskrit grammar is used for abundance also	It further indicates that Brahman is source of bliss and individual self is manifestation of it. Scripture denies blissful one or individual one being insentient or *Pradhana* and entity supreme (blissful) and individual are enjoined.
Gods (Sun, eyes, direction etc.) are different from individual self or *atman* are mentioned separately in *Upnishadic* text.	It mentions quality of Gods example – Sun with golden hairs, pink body, lotus eyes etc.

Word space or *Akasha*/ ether, In-breath or *Prana* and light is to be understood as Bhrahman as mentioned in *Upnishad*	All are mentioned based on abundance (Ether/light/air etc) from observers' point of view, but not be understood as brahman

Section II

Objection	**Refutation**
Brahman is the object of meditation as taught in *upnishad*, with the qualities justified in *vedic* text.	Embodied individual soul or *atman* is not referred here, as its quality do not fit for it like space in body, without speech, without any attachment etc. and identified with mind alone.
Mention of subject & object, which is to be attained by subject, hence one identified with mind is not individual self or *atman* or supreme soul or brahman, which are two different entities.	It is impossible to assert all pervasiveness of something which is spatially limited like self or *atman* within the heart and subtle, however we can say other way as omnipresent to have limited presence in some way of existence, like king of world rules certain place also.
Eye is appropriate seat of God as mentioned in *upnishad*	It sounds logical as God is untouched by all blemishes like sin etc. so as eye is untarnished by blemishes of text and water or clarified butter poured in eye will flow out from eyelid.
Brahman is said to be omnipresent like space	Brahman is without name, form or any qualities but for the sake of

(Ether), how can it have specific place at the same time as eye, earth etc.	meditation symbols are presented in text.
Person in eye is God, but not supreme self and is known for the path of God followed by person with knowledge	It is for the reference to the vision of enlightened man and for the purpose of inducing aspirant to meditation.
Entity possessed with qualities of not being seen, without source, features etc. is Brahman and have characteristic like omniscient etc., embodied soul or *atman* with limited adjunct cannot be omniscient etc.	Brahman alone is the source of all being not *pradhana* or elements, or individual soul, while purusha or supreme self is transcendental, formless, coextensive, birthless without vital forces etc. and way to know him is by presentation of its form as the source of all things.
Vaisvanara or cosmic person is supreme lord though the two words *Vaisvanara* & self, denote many things but used in *upnishad* in specifically as supreme lord as indicatory only.	Instructions in *upnishad* is to conceive Brahman but specification mentioned does not fit to any other things and reason *upnishad* mentions him as *purusa* or supreme self since *Vaisvanara* or cosmic person is neither a deity nor an element, while spatial limitations are for the sake of meditation based on superimposition on formless.

Section III

Upnishad states "supreme self is repository of heaven, earth etc. and the one without second and holds everything like string holding all, when all desire dwells in heart are gone the mortal being becomes immortal & attains Brahman in this very body", while there is no common ground to establish inference with anything else to prove Bhraman like *pradhana* (insentient material elements) or any sentient element, where *upnishad* mentions difference between knowable object and knower and sentient object cannot be repository since it itself is seeker.

There is no firm rule to know Brahman, like being size of thumb in heart, light, ether, plentitude etc. *Badarayna* author of *Bharma sutra* says scripture sanctions competency even for divine being like Gods etc. to know Brahman, as priest & others on one side and *Indra or* king of Gods and others divine being on other side participate in rituals will be incompatible in ritualistic point of view since priest and God's seeking for same thing.

It is said in *upnishad* that being in sleep and one who departs body (at death) are different, during sleep supreme lord or brahman is mentioned separate from embodied soul or *atman*, which is fully embraced by supreme self and supreme self is not the subject of transmigration.

Section IV

Objection	**Refutation**
Inferred entity is *pradhana* or elements mentioned in some part of *upnishad*	To chalk out path of liberation from worldly state by comparison of body and rest, whereas subtle state or Causal state is meant by unmanifested or *Avyakta* & for entity not to be known, *upnishad* does not explicitly mention *avyakta* as element or *padartha*, however it is understood from the context it is used.

Brahman is presented in all *upnishad* as the cause of space and all other manifestation but has diverged ways like emerged from space, started from light, begun with vital forces etc.	There is no difference in regard to brahman as creator, nonexistence does not mean void because of its allusion to brahman. *Upnishad* says that self is to be realized and profoundly to be meditated upon which is supreme self or brahman. Meaning is derived from correlation of passage of *upnishad* and statement of non-difference between individual self or *atman* and supreme self or *brahman.*

Brahman must be material cause (like clay, gold etc. for making pot, ornaments etc.) as well as efficient cause (like potter, gold smith etc.) along with willingness to create as mentioned in *upnishad,* so creation of universe is action by him for himself by changing his own form and is the theory of cause of universe.

Chapter 2 – *Avirodha* or "Non contradiction"

Section I

Objection	Refutation
Brahman is the cause of universe which gives defect to the *smiritis* or text of one's experience where insentient elements or *pradhana* is independent cause of creation	God is reveled at number of places as material and efficient cause, with the help of *smiritis* it reinforces the point that brahman is material and efficient cause of universe and

	confirmed in *yoga* philosophy also.
Product like gold ornament cannot have clay in it as both have different material cause, dissimilar material cannot be produced from similar material, similarly for universe with diverse manifestation of insentient being are formed from insentient which should be brahman.	Insentient deities (vision, sound, direction etc.) identifying themselves with (earth, sun etc.) are referred to as engaged in activity befitting conscious being (speaking, seeing, etc.) not the organs or elements are alluded to. It is observed that insentient being (nail, hair etc.) grows from sentient being and other way sentient being growing from insentient (scorpion growing from cow dung) are seen
The effect that is universe, which is unconscious, impure and with attributes (sound etc.) was nonexistent before creation and the cause (bhrahman) free from attributes are then by belief of preexistence of effect is not justified.	Denial cannot amount to rejection of existence before creation. Even today, effect has existence only with reference to material cause, so it has existence in that vey way before creation.
During dissolution effect becomes cause and it will taint the cause with its attributes and brahman becomes tainted which is incongruous	Though the effect merges to cause, it does not pollute it, like products (pot, ornaments etc.) fashioned out of material like clay or gold when getting

	absorbed they do not transfer their features.
Distinction between experiencer or *bhokta* for happiness, sorrow etc. and to be experienced object or *bhogya* will cease when the object of experience turns to experiencer.	It is observed that foam, ripples, waves, bubble are modification of water and not different from water, similarly experiencer and object are never identified by each other, nor they are different from brahman. On account of *upnishad* it is cited that knowledge of all, is followed up by the knowledge of one (when clay is known, all modifications as pot, plate, vases etc. are known), universe is effect, diversified as space etc. and cause is supreme self (brahman), in reality effect is not different from cause. It is established that, effect can be perceived only (ornament, pot, cloth etc.) not cause (gold, clay, yarn etc.), and cause must exist before effect hence the brahman (cause) was never without existence in all periods of time.

It is inferred that effect (universe etc.) did not exist before creation (manifestation) as stated in *upnishad.*	Nonexistence of effect does not mean absolute nonexistence of effect, although effect does exist as non-different from cause before creation (cloth does exist in yarn but undifferentiated) however from standpoint of difference it was nonexistent, preexistence and non-difference are spoken in *upnishad.*
All effect was non- different from each other and these facts do not fit in before creation. As curd is not from clay and pot is not from milk	Certain potency (milk to become curd) existed, for in breath or *prana* which takes different form of vital forces is undifferentiated when breathed have potency to become vital force.
Individual soul or *atman* is mentioned identical with brahman or supreme soul, hence individual soul being creator should not create unpleasant things like death, old age etc.	Brahman being higher then embodied being and to brahman beneficial things does not arise since it has no benefit to be achieved or harmful to be eschewed which is eternally free with analogy of stone (all born from earth some are valuable like diamond/ rare earth and other are dust) same way individual soul has defects.
Brahman cannot be a lone cause of creation since creation requires causal means (like potter needs	It is possible to create with the analogy of milk turning to curd or water into ice without external accessories and in this

clay, wheel, rod etc. to create pot) but brahman is without help hence creation by him alone is not possible.	way Gods, sentient and insentient were created by brahman.
There arises contingency of entire brahman transforming to creation as partial transformation is not possible since brahman is without parts and it will be of transforming entirely, hence after creation there will be no brahman outside creation.	Authority of *upnishad* need to be accepted which states power of brahman which is beyond thoughts and can be understood though *vedas* only. *Upnishad* states diverse creation occurs to the individual soul or *atman* in dream without change of nature (there is no chariot no animal to them but creates all), similarly there can be a diverse creation by brahman without changing its nature.
Scripture states brahman is without organ then how can he perform action of creation, even if it is omnipotent.	Brahman can be known though *vedas* only not by reasoning and all distinctions are derived from him alone, still it can have accession of all power in all aspect which is conjured by himself.
There can be no motive to brahman to create, since creation of universe with multiple conglomerations of high and low things is a huge task	It is pastime for brahman like king with all desire fulfilled may indulge in activities likes sports, stadiums etc.

<table>
<tr><td>Brahman can be charged for partiality like creation of Gods, humans, animals, misery, happiness etc. and of cruelty like disease, death etc. since brahman being the creator.</td><td>As rainfall is common cause of growth of paddy, barley etc. based on potential of individual seed, similarly brahman is common cause of creation of Gods, humans, animals etc. while individual fruit of work associated with individual creature are uncommon cause for the diverse creation, hence brahman has no partiality or cruelty.</td></tr>
<tr><td>Merit or demerit of karma cannot be taken into account at creation since it was undistinguished in beginning.</td><td>It is stated in upnishad that transmigration has no beginning.</td></tr>
<tr><td colspan="2">Brahman is accepted as cause of all creation and its characteristics of cause as omniscient, omnipresent, omnipotent, great conjurer etc. fits for it.</td></tr>
</table>

Section II

Objection	Refutation
It can be Inferred that, elements or *pradhana* is the cause of universe since brahman is not perceivable, and something perceivable cannot come from not perceivable things	It is impossible since • Insentient things unless guided by sentient being cannot produce modifications (clay to pot) and there is no inherent tendency in insentient to create. • Spontaneity like flow of milk, water etc. for the insentient cannot happen unless guided. • Nothing else existed before creation and no external help to *pradhana* or elements to impel creation • The occurrence of an event at one place (grass converting to milk in cow) and nonoccurrence at other places (grass not converting to milk in bull) cannot happen unless there is divine intervention.
Cause of creation is atom, which continues to exist after dissolution of universe and various magnitudes are produced from multiplicity	Combination of various actions is contingent of action, since action is an effect, hence some cause which needs to be assumed.

of this cause which is an atom	During dissolution no initial action will occur to an atom and all the actions are possible after creation hence an atom cannot be a cause.
Inherence theory of dyad, or originating from combination of two different kinds of atoms, which is entirely different from constituent atom, and it inherits both of them as *pradhana* or element	It will lead to infinite regress, since dyad are connected through relationship of inherence of constituent atoms, and which is entirely different from inhering component which will be connected through separate relation by nature of inherence, so similarity of absolute difference will exist which will lead to successive relationship and other relationship and so on.
Atoms are active, inactive, both active and inactive, neither active nor inactive are the basis of explanation of creation and dissolution	Active – dissolution not possible Inactive – creation not possible Active and inactive – not reconcilable owing to contradiction Neither active nor inactive – then two must originate from same cause, if cause is known then it will lead to constant activity with no dissolution and without cause it will be inactive with no creation

Atoms are the last limit of process of breaking up of composite things and atoms are of four kinds based on qualities it possesses. Atoms as constituent and modification endowed with qualities are the cause of creation and atoms are considered as eternal	Atoms becoming grosser and less eternal is absurd, and it will lead to impermanency also. Modification containing certain kinds of atom with certain quality will be in abundance in gross form and all elements have part of some qualities like earth having quality of water and so on.
Combination or integration of two different kinds of elements (arising out of combination of atom) can create	Such combination will be insentient, and consciousness can flash by the contact of sense organs, and it is possible only to the sentient being, hence creation by integration of elements is not possible.
No sentient and steady experiencer is admitted as an agent which brings combination of elements still the transmigratory *atman* or individual soul existence is possible due to ignorance (permanence, delusion, names, form, sense, birth, death, sorrow, wailing, pain etc.) and rest are cause of one another, if transmigratory existence is possible then there is no need to depend on other	They are just a cause of origination of one another, a combination (cause & effect) may be possible but cannot be ascertained, ignorance may be the cause of one another but nothing can become possibly the source of combination (they themself have to emerge into being depending on combination), if postulated for cause and effect is considered then relationship cannot be established since succeeding activity will obliterate the proceeding one.

agent as cause and effect of one another. With such combination of things, where creation is emerging out by force of circumstances then creation is possible, without brahman	
How can an effect arise, when there is no cause	Then anything may originate from anywhere and the entity of earlier moment continues till origination of later moment and cause and effect will be simultaneous.
Object of knowledge is in three categories *Paritishmkhy nirodha* – artificial annihilation *Apritisamkhya nirodha* – natural annihilation *Akasha* – absence of obstruction	These two kinds of annihilation are not possible and there cannot be a cessation which is perceivable in chain of causality or the individual (forming the chain), chain cannot cease since individual forming chain continues as succession of cause and effect hence annihilation of eighter kind is untenable. *Akasha* is an entity that can be known through *vedic* text (*Akasha* originating from self)
All things are momentary	In that case, the perceiver also needs to be momentary but by the fact of remembrance (recalling by mind after perception) it is not seen, hence

	not possible and it is only possible when agents of perception and memory are same.
Things come out of nothing	Not possible even in general experience, otherwise success should come to indifferent people without effort.
External things which cannot be perceived do not exist	It cannot be said what is not perceived does not exist, like certain frequency of waves are not perceived by humans, it does not mean it do not exist.
Perception of things in waking and dream state are different in nature, one is perception and the other is memory. In absence of objects in sleep, diversity of experience can be explained basis tendencies or Impressions or *samskara*	Tendencies cannot arise when object is not perceived, if tendencies have no beginning, then chain of one tendency creating another will start from initial defect that first tendency created without external object, then it will be like blind leading the blind
Ego or I-consciousness is assumed to be unchanging by nature.	Doctrine of momentariness is not possible unless there is some principle running through everything and abiding through all period of time or unchanging witness.
Belief is of two categories "soul" and "non soul" and all	It is impossible for one to present and another does not, it is a contradictory

are included as best they can in these two. Logic of seven facts – somehow exist, somehow does not exist, somehow exist and somehow does not exist, somehow indescribable, somehow exist and indescribable, somehow does not exist and indescribable, somehow exist or does not exist and indescribable.	characteristic, as existence and nonexistence and so on, are associated simultaneously with the same thing just as cold and heat cannot be same time at one place.
Embodied souls have dimensions of body	In that case soul cannot be omnipotent and body has no fixed dimension that changes with stage of growth (infant/ youth etc.) in same life but the *atman* or individual soul do not change
Bondage and liberation are expressed as surrounded by *karma* and remains sunk in the sea of world is like bottle gourd remains sunk in water till bonded to its branch, which floats when bondage is snapped	In that case mutability becomes unavoidable for the soul or *atman*, which will be subjected to changes, depending on condition like piece of leather and will lead to impermanence of soul or *atman*.
God is not a material cause but just an efficient cause, where *Praktri* or nature is	In that case there can be no causality towards universe and brahman being just a superintendent over material

material cause & *Purusha* or soul being efficient cause	and soul, in that case lord by creating creatures into grades of inferiority, mediocrity and superiority will be subjected to like and dislike then he ceases to be a God. Whereas brahman acts in accordance with the past action or *karma* of creature which makes God only an impeller, which is logical, people serve others, when compelled by their own interest which is defect incase applied to God & God cease to be God in that case, so the God is special kind of soul (*purusha*) which is indifferent to everything.
God or brahman is different from individual soul or *atman* and nature, and it cannot rule unless they have some kind of relationship with soul and nature, which is not possible since nature, individual soul or *atman* & God or brahman are all omnipresent, part less nor have relationship of inherence and it is impossible to determine what contains what.	

Objection	**Refutation**
Since all arguments are based on scripture, then other schools of thoughts are also composed by revered teachers, hence should be accepted	Knowledge from scripture which has authority of being omniscience of author are *vedas*, whereas scriptures by others are by one or few authors.

God imagined by sophist, is that he could impel nature or *padhartha* or elements to create as potter in case of clay	It cannot be established, since it is beyond the range of perception and nature is devoid of any form. It will result in God becoming experiencer as happiness, sorrow etc. which is not possible
God cannot be proved since no physical support is possible to him as king having a body is able to rule kingdom	Such analogy is not possible in case of God, since body or support came into being after creation
It is assumed that God or brahman is equipped with sense organs	It is impossible since God or brahman do not undergo any experience like transmigrating soul or *atman*, otherwise we will be faced with predicament of God or brahman himself being deprived of Godhood
God or brahman is conceived as omniscient as well infinite, so as the nature and individual soul or *atman*, which all are different from one another, can this limit (number of extensions) of nature and soul, to be determined by God.	Nature, soul and he or brahman will come to an end, if limits in number is grasped by God or brahman, anything with limitation eventually comes to an end
God or brahman as *Vasudeva* or all-pervading lord, who is pure consciousness by	*Narayna* being higher than nature is agreed, but with regard to other (*samkarsana*,

nature is supreme reality, he divided himself and set himself in four fold figure as *Vasudeva* -God, *samkarsana* – individual soul or *atman*, *pradyumma* – mind and *anirudda* – ego or I-concious, as material cause, and by acquiring requisite form of worship to him one attains lord himself which is *Vasudeva*	*aniruddha and pradumma*) originating from him is not possible, it will lead to impermanence if individual soul with beginning and end logic, whereas *veda* defines individual soul has no origin. It is never seen that implement originating from agent of action by cutting in parts

Section III

Refuting doubt on creation by various *upnishads*, as each are complimenting other and self- contradiction clarified

Action	Explanation
Insentient being Origen of space	• *Upnishadic* passage on creation of space is in secondary sense like "make a space" in room or "make a space" in box, where space is not a creation but of perpetual existence • All creation originates from inherent (material) and noninherent (concomitant) and efficient cause, inherent cause must have been in abundance of the same class, but for space there is

	none and action of efficient cause is not possible. • All creation has peculiarity before and after creation (fire- illumination after creation) but none in case of space • In *upanisadic* text while comparing brahman with space with respect to attributes of omnipresence and eternity "self is to be known as space or all pervasive as space
Origen of air	Extending the above logic of space to air, as air gets support from space it is automatically explained
Origen of brahman denied	Unless primary cause is admitted, it will all lead to infinite regress, beginningless need to be accepted which is brahman, other cause being primordial is negated
Origen of fire	Brahman is the source of fire, it is said "in beginning it was existence alone and that created fire, and everything originated from him"
Origen of water	Water born from fire no objection

Origen of earth Word food means earth (*vedic* text) as in *upnishad* "water deliberated, let me be many and created food"	It refers to rain not earth, since rain is synonyms to food
Creation by God deliberation	• He performed meditation on each of the things and created is by *upnishad*, it is known from indicatory mark that "he who inhabitant of earth is within it, and to whom earth does not know, but body is the earth and controls earth from within" • Elements have activity only when they are presided over by someone and for all creation there is no other witness but him
Reverse order of dissolution	It is logical that dissolution is reverse order of creation- earth originating from water should end at its period in water and water from fire returns to fire and eventually mergers to brahman
Sentient being Origen of mind and intellect	Intellect and mind find accommodation in some intermediate stage, it has

	evidence and mentioned in scripture. Presence of intellect and mind do not disturb order of creation or dissolution
Birth and death	Birth and death are in primary sense as motion and motionlessness, but for soul it is for secondary sense as body is present or not, since individual soul has no origin hence soul has no birth or death
Origen of soul	Individual soul has no origin as living in cage of body as jiva with senses becomes associated with fruit of work or *karma*
Eternally conscious soul	Soul being free from origin and dissolution is eternal as cognizer
Dimension of soul	• Individual soul or *atman*, must be of atomic dimension as stated in *vedas*, it departs from body and goes to another world by following certain course and returns back from there • Movement of individual soul or *atman* within the body is stated as "completely withdrawing he comes to heart and taking a shining

	organ with him, he comes again to waking state" which is possible for atomic size only
"Self or *atman*, which is great and birthless identified with intellect only is in midst of organ" is mentioned in *upnishad*, if it means that embodied soul possessed of vast dimension	It is referred in different context in dealing with supreme self or brahman, as chief reality to be known and atomic size of individual soul or *atman* is not contradicted, like sandal wood paste in contact with one part of body produces sensation all over the body same way soul though located in one part will have perception all over body
Analogy of sandal paste accepted, but not precepted in case of soul	• Place of individual soul or *atman* is accepted in *upnishad* at heart • The quality of sentient being is pervasive, it is atomic in size and like lamp in corner of room illuminate entire room
As smell being quality of substance can have separate existence – smell of sandal can be perceived even when sandal wood is not in view	Individual soul or *atman* being an atomic in size and its quality of being sentient can be detached to it, as *upnishad* says "from tip of hair to tip of nail soul pervades"
Soul or *atman* and intelligence are separate	• Soul or *atman* is identified by modes of intellect

since taught separately in *upnishad*	(desire, like, dislike etc.) these modes constitute essence or chief factor in attainment of transmigration or freedom, still it comes to have state of being an agent and experiencer which is caused by superimposition of modes to intellect as limiting adjunct. It is stated in scripture "association between soul or *atman* and intellect persist till worldly state (transmigration) of soul continues" • Association of soul with intellect remains latent or dormant in sleep and dissolution, which manifest during waking state or at creation • If existence of internal organ (*manas*- faculty of thinking, *buddhi* – faculty of knowing, *ujnana* – cognation / ego, *chitta* – feeling or memory) is admitted then possibility of constant perception or non-perception with the power of soul or *atman* is lost

Soul as an agent	• Scriptural injunctions mention, action as "one should perform sacrifice, pour oblations, make gifts etc." are purposeful only when it assigns duty to actual agent • Scriptural text says "it roams in intermediate state or dream and goes wherever it likes and moves as it please in its own body" hence it is an agent performing task • Soul though independent with regard to the perception of good and bad with no rule applicable to it, but not in matter related to activity yielding result, for which it is dependent on space, time & agent and does not cease to have its agent ship depending on accessories, like chef depends on accessories for cooking, which is an agent only to chef • *Samadhi* or deep meditation taught in *upnishad* as means of realization of self, it is

	possible only when soul is an agent of meditation
Soul under condition	• It is not possible for the soul to have natural agent ship otherwise it will negate liberation • Causal activity (merit/ demerit etc.) becomes connected to agent (soul) and activity invokes its power when connected this way and becomes impossible to get rid of it entirely • Soul when associated with limiting adjunct are called enjoyer – state of being an agent and an experience are conjured by ignorance as duality to see one another, but for knower of brahman everything becomes self.
Soul agent ship derived from God	• Individual soul impelled by like, dislike etc. endowed with all action can have experiences of agent ship and God has no role in it • God takes into account of effort for virtuous or vicious deeds which individual makes, and God acts as instrument only, like rain

	falling equally to all, hence individual agent ship depends on God but still it is individual who acts, God directs soul based on past deeds and transmigratory existence which is without beginning
Relation of God with individual soul is like master and servant or like fire and spark	• Supreme self or brahman is not touched by suffering of individual soul or *atman* as light not affected by things it illuminates • Individual soul or *atman* is only reflection of supreme self or brahman, like reflection of sun in water, if one reflection moves other may not, similarly if one individual soul becomes associated with certain *karma*, other may not, hence results are not intermixed

Section IV

Action	Explanation
Origen of vital forces or *prana*	• *Prana* or vital breath are produced from supreme self or brahman, scriptural text says "from self emanates all organs, all world, all gods and all being" • Origen of *prana* must be accepted since it is impossible to have term origin used in secondary sense
Number of *pranas* or vital breath – various numbers are mentioned It is mentioned as seven, or eight *prana & grahas* - perceiver of sense organ, nine – seven in head and two below, ten- nine organ & neval, eleven – ten as a before and mind, twelve, thirteen etc.	It is seven, because organ of head, hands and other places mentioned in *upnishad* in addition to seven are *grahas* or senses controlled by *atigrahas* or object of senses
Size of *prana* or vital breath is atomic in size	*Prana* is atomic in size which is beyond perception (seeing, feeling etc.) but not like ultimate atom otherwise body activity will be impossible

Though *prana* is all pervasive but functions only in body, and soul to be of atomic size owing to association with *pranas*	*Pranas* are *karanas* (cause serving to produce effect) like eye is *karana* to vision, hence it will not be all pervasive and is asserted that *prana* are subtle and limited in size
Creation of *prana*	*Brahman* is creator of *prana*
Nature of *prana*	*Prana* is neither an air nor its function, but is a cosmic energy
General view is that *prana* is air and of four kinds (outgoing breath, incoming breath, spreads in body & moves upward), and it combines with organ of senses to produce activity	• *Prana* and sense organ are taught separately & *prana* being a quadrant of brahman, it shines and scatters heat (manifest in its own sphere), had it been from air alone, it would not been mentioned separately from air, where *prana* is separately spoken as an activity of sense organ (speech etc.) • *Prana* is not independent like soul also, since instructions are imparted to it for the reason of sense organs as subservient to soul which enables its agent ship and an experiencer • *Prana* has five state like mind *(prana, apana, vyana, udana & samana)* this distinction of state is due to

	different activity performed by each one of it
Scripture says that presiding deities or sense organs, like fire and other can engage in their work by virtue of power they themselves posses	Sense organs are connected to possessor of sense organs through deities presiding over the *prana*, but are related to embodied soul or *atman* which is possessor of vital forces (I smell this is by soul, and senses of smell is for sake of smelling by it) Embodied soul or *atman* being an experiencer has constant relation with body (based on *karma*), although deities presiding over *prana*, yet the embodied soul or *atman* does not cease to an experiencer, where deity are classified with sense organs, but not with experiencer soul
Prana and *pranas* – other *pranas* are mode of chief *prana* or an independent reality	Chief *prana* and other *prana* (eleven in number) are designated as organs. *Upnishad* states chief *prana* and sense organs are different (speech etc.) and by dissimilarity in characteristic also, when sense organ goes for sleep, like sight, speech etc., then chief *prana* awakes, and it

	is beyond grasp of death at the time of sleep
Creation of gross object	Taught in *upnishad* • Arrangement of designations (manifestation of name and form) is by chief *prana* who makes elements tripartite (mixer of fire, water and earth) • Flesh etc. are produced from earth and other two parts of food consumed are divided in three parts gross – excreta, medium- flash & subtle – mind

Chapter 3 –Transmigration

Section I

Action	**Explanation**
Transmigratory soul or *atman* moves out of body without mixed subtle elements which are seed for next body	It is stated in *vedas* that, in the matter of obtaining next body, individual soul or *atman* moves out enveloped by subtle elements
Upnishad says, soul or *atman* moves out accompanied with water alone	It is not the water alone, water has component of fire, water and earth with water as predominant, it refers to performance of rituals and associated with them, as

	oblation is assumed subtle and in potential form, moves about virtue of substances in soul called faith (result of rituals) Faith along with impression of past, is poured as oblation in heaven to produces lunar body
Sense organs do not accompany soul or *atman* at time of death of body and as scripture says that sense organs enter into respective deities like vocal to fire etc.	*Upnishad* says that, when soul or *atman* depart vital forces or *prana* follow and when vital forces depart sense organs follows. It is used in secondary sense and merger is figurative (it is not logical for hair or head to fly by its own to reach tree etc.), hence fire and other deities presiding over speech etc. are helping them in their activity and ceases to favor them at the time of death.
Soul does not depart enveloped by water	It is perceived to be so, in case of those performing rituals, it is shown that one performing ritual reaches moon preceding along smoke "path of manes" for which king is soma and oblation is faith
Soul or *atman* becomes food to God as mentioned in *upnishad*, so there cannot be a rebirth	It is used in a metaphorical sense, it relates to enjoyment of companionship of those who perform rituals

It is stated in text that those with noble action after death, proceed along the path of smoke "to reach lunar world and enjoys fruit of their work till *karma* is reached to end and returns by the same route along with residual *karma*"

Doubt	**Explanation**
Are all *karma* enjoyed before returning to mortal world or have some residual *karma* at return	*Karma* consumed are conducive to heaven and remanent are at return like pot of oil is not emptied entirely when poured out
Soul or *atman* get rebirth owing to conduct not residual *karma*	Conduct is used suggestively for residual *karma*, since *karma* is dependent on conduct. Action eighter good and evil are referred directly by *karma* as performance of action and are synonyms word
Vedic text says moon is goal even for the performer of unholy act	• Ascent to moon is meant for experience of *karma*, not a transit for descent, those who do not perform holy act have no experience at moon • They enter place of death or hell and suffer torment in accordance to their misdeed and ascend to this world as explained in *upnishad* (*Nachiketa* section) • Records in *simirits* (*Mahabharat* etc.), it is noticed that there are four

	kinds of life which are viviparous, oviparous, life from moisture and plant later two are born without mating hence oblation are overlooked
Descending soul attains similarity with space	It resorts reverse path as they have gone to moon, that is Space – air—smoke—vapor—cloud—pour as rain
Time lag between each of the states are not mentioned	Time lag is short, from space to rain and forming paddy etc.
Soul or *atman* becoming paddy, herbs, tree etc. after being part of rain, does soul experience suffering/ happiness of the plant which are natural to plants	Soul or *atman* merely comes in contact of paddy etc. which are already inhabited by others soul and do not share happiness / suffering etc. with that soul. After becoming paddy etc., as scripture state that soul becomes progenitor and become one with the consumer of food and perform act of generation and from womb comes a new body for descending soul.

Section II

As per *unpinshad*, real creation occurs during intermediate state or dream state

Doubt	**Explanation**
Creation in dream state is illusionary	Creation during dream state must not be real, self or *atman* is the creator of desired things during dream, but creation is *maya* or illusionary since it is not a complete manifestation of all attributes found in waking state
Dream is an omen also, which is indication of good and evil fortune	Meditation on supreme lord or brahman, to manifest something which remains obscured otherwise because soul bondage and freedom are derived from brahman and individual soul or *atman* being a part of brahman as "spark and fire" is associated with brahman, hence gets omens
Soul in deep sleep	Dreamless sleep takes place in nerve, and all sense organs withdrawn and becomes completely serene in mind, but individual soul or *atman* remains spread over these nerves.
On who awakes after merger or deep sleep, are the	Aphorism says it is the same soul which goes for deep sleep

same soul or other entity as no such rules are specified	returns back, it can be reconfirmed by • Unfinished action- one cannot engage in work incomplete by other, it will have unwarranted conclusion • Remembrance – one remembers the things after waking for the things of event before sleep
Soul in swoon – unconscious man could be a fifth state, as four states are waking, dream, deep sleep & departure	It is a state when one is partially sleep and partially other state and are at door of death, so long its *karma* last, his speech and mind returns from swoon otherwise it departs and knower of brahman call this state as partial sleep not the fifth state
Nature of brahman- its qualification/ attributes	Vedic text says brahman is with and without qualification or adjuncts
Characteristic with and without attributes	Logically it cannot have contradictory characteristic, when it is in association with limiting adjunct and substance of different kind, that can change its nature (transparent crystal cannot become opaque when in contact with red color, and an illusion of red color

	crystal is an error), brahman has one characteristic of attribute less and it is unchanging
Brahman mention in *upnishad* is with attributes as "has four feet (quarters or directions)" or "sixteen digits (parts)"	• Scripture negates each of the differences individually, differences spoken are for sake of meditation and non-difference is real purport of scripture and does not support diverse aspect • Certain section favors realization of non-duality after condemning dualistic teaching, "formless for sure" like beam of light, falling on object to create form and brahman are meditated on those forms created • Brahman as pure consciousness devoid of any other aspect and distinguishing features • Self or *atman* by nature is pure consciousness, with distinctness beyond speech and mind, it can be taught by way of negating other things, hence scripture dealing with liberation has

	illustration cited as "like sun reflects in water"
Material things as water is remotely placed from material things like sun to form an image, hence two material things are needed whereas supreme self is not a material entity	This illustration is apt so far point conveyed is pertinent, reflection of sun is water increases with increase in size of water and moves when water moves and differs when water differs thus the sun confirms characteristic of water, but in reality, sun never has any of these, similarly while brahman remains unchanging and retaining its sameness seems to confirm limiting adjunct of body
Unconditioned brahman	*Upnishad* denies all limitation in describing brahman, "not so, not so" because there is no other appropriate description and "not so" use of word is to indicate connection with something in proximity also *Upnishad* further says brahman is unmanifested hence cannot be comprehended through perception (eye etc.) or can be attained through *karma*, since it is in unmanifested form Brahman is realized only in *smadhai or* deep meditation, as stated in *upnishad*

Entity meditated upon and the meditator are two separate entities, which is supreme self or brahman and individual self or *atman*	Effulgent self or brahman appears to be different during meditation activity but intrinsically there is no difference and is evident from text, where it is repeated several times. Non-difference is natural to brahman, and difference is due to ignorance which is destroyed through knowledge and attains unity with supreme self which is brahman and *atman* Indicatory marks in *upnishad* are "anyone knows brahman, becomes brahman himself", "being brahman is being absorbed in brahman" Difference (subject and object of meditation) and non-difference between self or *atman* and brahman are established which is like snake and its coil (snake in coil, hood, stretch look different but a same snake) and light and its source both are effulgent but are not different
Bharman is one without second, while *upnishad*	Mention of embankment is for the sake of intellectual grasp,

mentions words like "embankment, magnitude, connection and difference", it means there is another entity above that	magnitude of brahman is mentioned as embankment that all is contained within it Mention of connections is in context to differences mentioned about brahman from the point of view of limiting adjunct like the case of light, where light from sun/ moon etc. undergo diversity owing to the contact with conditioning factor but becomes united when factor is removed These limitations are logically justified, and denial of everything else follows after that
Fruit of action eighter, it springs from action itself or from God	Fruit of action should be from God, since he presides over everything and aware of specific creation and time conducive for different creation/ preservation/ dissolution, he should ordain fruit of work to people according to merit or demerit mentioned in *upnishad*

Section III

<table>
<tr><th>Doubt</th><th>Explanation</th></tr>
<tr><td>All kinds of meditation are same is imparted in all upnishad</td><td>Concept of meditation or Vijnana is same since it has similar injunctions in all upnishads</td></tr>
<tr><td>There is difference in details of vijnana or meditation in different upnishad</td><td>Though certain traits are added or deducted from entity to be meditated upon, yet meditation is recognized to be the same</td></tr>
<tr><td colspan="2">Combination of traits in of any the meditation type, mentioned in any one upnishad must be combined with similar meditation everywhere since its application is not different in any kind of meditation</td></tr>
<tr><td colspan="2">Difference of meditation – there is no difference of udgitha meditation mentioned in chandogyay upnishad and bradhiryankya upnishad, meditation differ owing to difference in introductory sentence</td></tr>
<tr><td colspan="2">Word OM pervades in all vedas, and it is appropriate to qualify OM as udgitha or loud recitation</td></tr>
<tr><td colspan="2">Sameness of meditation on prana – all meditation on prana being same, but attributes to be meditated upon in section of upnishad to be added in another section mentioned elsewhere</td></tr>
<tr><td>Attributes of meditation to be accepted, as they appear separately under different context in upnishad</td><td>All characteristics of brahman as bliss etc. are to be understood as belonging to all context in meditation</td></tr>
<tr><td>Characteristics mentioned in upnishad like “having joy</td><td>No, since such characteristic have intensity of degree but</td></tr>
</table>

as head", "enjoyment is right side", "hilarity on left side" etc. are to be accepted everywhere	brahman is without difference (one without second)
Attributes of brahman (bliss, consciousness, omnipresent etc.) is to be accepted in context to certain places but not every where	Characteristics of brahman are to be understood as belonging to everywhere since it is equally substantiating everywhere, hence attributes exist collectively everywhere
Kath upnishad mentions that "senses object are higher than senses and mind is higher than senses object, but nothing is higher than *purusha*"	It is reasonable that *purusha* is higher than all but not each one propounding to be higher to one another, since it does not serve any purpose of relative superiority
Aitaraya upnishad mentions that "in beginning it was self alone ", one referred is supreme self or someone else	Supreme self is brahman and to be understood as self everywhere in *upnishad*
Meditation on self, which is identified with mind having vital force, effulgent appearance, resplendent within the heart like grain of rice etc.	Meditation is same, and attributes is to be combined, it is precisely through the presentation of similar trait in all text, when a sentence serves purpose by presenting something not known earlier and something known are logically held as restatement of fact

<table>
<tr><td colspan="2">In case of meditation attributes need to combine, since it has same connection with object of meditation</td></tr>
<tr><td colspan="2">Attributes of brahman such as possession of unchallenged power, pervasion in heaven etc., are not to be added in meditation since, its association with abode cannot lead to oneness with self, further no rituals should be part of meditation eighter</td></tr>
<tr><td>Path of God after destruction of good and evil are followed differently, which emerges sometimes and sometime not, to the follower of qualified (sagun) and non-qualified (nirgun) brahman</td><td>Soul course after death must have purposefulness in two ways, both should emerge differently (in accordance with knowledge of brahman) which is not available invariably to all.

Differentiation is for knower of brahman whose all desires are fulfilled, and seeds of evil are burnt while living here in this world and have nothing else to look for and journey is meaningless for them, while journey of soul along the path of Gods is not restricted to any kind of meditation and applies to all kind of meditation</td></tr>
<tr><td>Man with knowledge dies and does not get another body</td><td>No, since one with corporal existence and engaged in mission of wellbeing of world is regulated by mission, hence liberation comes inevitably to man of knowledge</td></tr>
</table>

All negative conception of immutable are to be combined like "cannot be perceived/ grasped", "neither gross nor subtle" etc. since all are presented in similar way	
Reciprocal reading of scripture, like "transmigrating soul as God and God as transmigrating soul" then soul gets an added excellence through its identity with God and God will have reduced stature	Reciprocatory is meant for meditation only, and process has to be applied to similar context where only one way is stated and as a result identified becomes virtually confirmed
"He who knows adorable, first born being which is *hirayangarbha* as *satya* brahmam", what is *satya* or thuth	Trail of *satya* is borrowed to other *upnishad* as rituals (*Jyotistoma*, *udgitha* etc.) thus meditation differ owing to the difference in context and traits have separate application
There is no obligatory rule that meditation is connected to *vedic* rituals, and it is obvious from *upnishad*, where no such limitations is stated, eliminating hindrances of rituals	
Meditation on *prana* or vital forces and *vayu* or air are same but represents different aspects of meditation which differs in accordance to divine and corporal context	
Meditation connected with accessories of rituals are not to be confined to the branch of *vedas* from which it has reference but are to be adopted in all branches of *vedas* as *mantra* or aphorism	
Meditation is different when there is difference in terminology as different characteristic attributed to different context, difference in result, difference of names & impossibility of combining all the characteristic	

Any form of meditation is accepted as alternate to same kind of meditation as it yields same result
Meditation based on symbol when undertaken, is for fulfilment of worldly desire and it may be combined or not combined with meditation on brahman, according to one's option, in eighter case result it will yield will be different
Upnishadic declaration that *OM* is an accessory to *vedic* rituals, and it is common to all *vedas*, on that basis it can coexist with meditation also, but is not obligatory to use *OM* in meditation

Section IV

Doubt	**Explanation**
Some school of thought is that "self or brahman holds subservient position in rituals, and result of knowledge is merely glorification of agent" that is knowledge is behavior of knower of brahman (In *upnishad* it states that, Janak performed sacrifice and distributed gifts, hence knowledge cannot be an independent outcome, as per text. Knowledge in association with rituals produces result and rituals are performed by knower of *vedas*	It is reveled in *upnishad* that supreme self or brahman is even greater than agent, which in this case is knowledge. In text it mentions that "whatever is done with knowledge" does not refer to all knowledge but confines to relevant meditation, that is part of topic of discussion, metaphorically, hundreds of objects can be distributed in multiple ways among two, so it the case with outcome by knowledge of performing rituals and gaining knowledge by meditation.

	Engagement with rituals is prescribed to one, merely to recite *vedas,* but these restrictive texts do not apply to men with knowledge since restrictions are made without any specification (with or without knowledge) and consent is accorded to religious act for glorification of knowledge and some refrain for religious act accordance to personal predilection. From knowledge comes destruction of entire world (which is creation of ignorance) and it belongs to monk who has no means to perform rituals and so they do not engage in rituals
Reminiscent of other stages is *sannyasa* or renunciation to worldly things	All stages of life is to be observed and *vedic* text speaks equally of all stages of life, and each stage has its purpose to be fulfilled
Text on *udgitha* or loud recitation etc. are just praise of meditation, because it is accepted as subservient to rituals	These injunctions are extraordinary text, and it becomes useless if considered for praise only, words used in aphorism are injunctive (one should meditate on *udgitha*)

Upnisdic stories are meant for ritualist applications (as *priplava* – priest telling stories during rituals)	Certain stories are specified for ritual purpose and priest relates stories like one beginning with *Manu* etc. All stories in *upnishad* are useless for *priplava* purpose, since *upnisidic* stories are meant for illustrating appropriate knowledge of meditation, people tend to forget concept, but if associated with stories are often not forgotten.
All ritual activities are necessary, and knowledge helps to perform duties at various stages of life, it is not appropriate to say knowledge does not depend on duty	Once knowledge of brahman has emerged, then it does not depend on any other factor, still a seeker after knowledge must endow with control of body and mind and other virtues, which is means of acquiring knowledge. Factors such as, being in control, calm and withdrawn to itself as compulsory to undertake as prescribed in rituals also.
As stated in aphorism, that there is no need for all duties at different stage of life, which are conducive to knowledge, but if man sticks to his own stage of life without desire of	Duties in order to life are to be performed, even for those not desirous of liberation as duty and knowledge are enjoined, having knowledge alone without duty is not

knowledge have no motivation to perform duty also	possible, which is true in eighter ways.
Lack of requisites like being a widow, handicap or lack of wealth etc., then one has no competency to knowledge	Person between two stages is entitled, and is mentioned in *upnishad*, *smritis* etc. and have special factors also available to the, as *japa* or repetition of divine names etc.
Man belonging to certain order of life which are *Brahmacharya* (student), *Gṛhastha* (householder), *Vanaprastha* (forest dweller/retiree), and *Sannyasa* (renunciate), have reversion from there	There is no reversion for it and there is restrictions to it, at the same time, no text allow reversion and have no fair procedure for it
Knowledge can be obtained in this life, if there is no obstructions as result of past work fruition and correct means are adopted	
Liberation is unform everywhere and there is no rule with regard result of liberation, because state is the same for all achieving it.	

Chapter 4 – Result

Section I

Mental repetition is necessary, and it is instructed repeatedly in *upnishad*, it have to culminate in intuitive realization of brahman by transfixing concept in mind.

Upnishad acknowledges brahman as self and had modes to understand this concept in various ways, meditation on symbol presented to aspirant should not identify himself as "mind of brahman" as himself, with symbol like gold can, corporal plane whereas meditation not identified with the kind of material plane "space as ornament or "sun as brahman".

Doubt	Explanation
Should the idea of higher be applied to lower or otherwise like "sun as brahman or brahman as sun"	Lower are to be looked upon as higher (sun as brahman) because of consequent exaltation of inferior one to be fancied as the higher like king's charioteer is honored as king himself
The idea of sun etc. is to be superimposed on subsidiary rituals (*udgitha* etc.) since it is reasonable, it is sanctified by being looked upon as sun etc. and rituals will be fruitful as sun etc., but it cannot be a part of rituals directly	
One should adore mentally while in sitting posture, since it is possible in that way only, it sets up current of similar thoughts and it is not possible while walking, running when mind is in motion or laying down when mind is in sleep, motionless clam mind is needed for uninterrupted flow of thoughts	
There is no specification on place of meditation, it can be taken up anywhere, where mind gets concentrated, and meditation is to be repeated till the moment of death as noticed in scripture	
After acquisition of knowledge of brahman, all opposite results (sin etc.) are removed	As declared in *upnishad*– "on realization, there occurs nonattachment and

	destruction of subsequent and previous sins"
Do the virtuous deeds after knowledge comes in play, since it has same origin as other deeds	Same way as other deeds, non-attachment happens to virtuous deeds also, and liberation follows as soon as body dies
After acquisition of knowledge of brahman, virtue and vices that have not begun to yield fruits (accumulated in past) are destroyed but also whose results are partially enjoyed are also destroyed	
Upnisdic text says that *vedic* rituals are meant for same result as the acquisition of knowledge of brahman	
When obligatory duties like *agnihotra* etc. are done for purpose of liberation, they become cause of exhausting sins and thereby purifying mind which is contributory to realization of brahman, where a*gnihotra* and other rituals when associated with meditation are better than one without it, it acquires certain distinctions owing to it, and have efficacy in producing knowledge of brahman	

Section II

Upnishad confirms that at time of death speech and other organs merges to mind and mind merges to vital forces or prana and vital forces withdraws and merges to individual soul or *atman* and departed soul stays with subtle elements (fire, water, space etc.) and constitute seed for the next body

Doubt	Explanation
If departure is same for enlightened and non-enlightened one	Path is the same for knower and ignorant one till the point of start of respective path of soul. Ignorant man continues resting on subtle elements with their seeds for next body under impulsion of past work or *karma* to the new body To the knower, sense organs do not depart from the body and individual soul, or *atman* is liberated and becomes immortal
Vital forces or *prana* and subtle elements of knower of brahman merges to supreme brahman and absorption to brahman is absolute with no remnants	
When soul of man who has realized qualified brahman is about to depart then illumination occurs at the top of heart and soul residing in heart departs through hundred and first nerve (top of head) owing to efficacy of knowledge and constant thought about the course, which is part of knowledge and proceed following the rays of sun. The soul departing at night continues to have connection with body, till the sun rays arrives and, same is the reason when sun is in the southern course.	

Section III

All journey of soul or *atman* start from flame, from there soul reaches to air in a year as specified in *upnishad* (opening to the size of chariot wheel etc.) and from sun it goes to moon and then through lightning, it gets connects to *varun* (water or rain)

Doubt	Explanation
Are flames etc. are marking on the path of journey or place of experience or conductor for carrying soul or *atman* to forward journey	They are conducting deities, due to their indicatory mark in *upnishad*, effect of deities is to escort soul or *atman* to their final destination Senses organs are bunched up owing to its separation from body, and sense organs being devoid of independent action, then deities being sentient is able to escort insentient ones which are sense organs.
Deity escorts soul or *atman* to conditioned brahman *hiryangarbha or* first manifestation or to the unconditioned brahman or unmanifested brahman	They are led to inferior conditioned brahman or *hiryangarbha*, since it has a locus, whereas for unconditioned brahman or unmanifested there is no such conception where it can approach as a goal and progress toward it as absolute brahman is omnipresent and is the innermost self of the traveler hence there is no need to take up journey

<table>
<tr><td></td><td>Designation of conditioned brahman or hirayangarbha is nearness to absolute brahman, so at the time of final dissolution of world, the conditioned brahman or hiryangarbha attain to unconditioned brahman, is known from upnisadic text and confirmed from smriti text also, however firm resolution about attainment is not concerned with conditioned brahman</td></tr>
<tr><td colspan="2">Superhuman being leads others to brahman only to those people, who do not use symbol in meditation, since it has two-fold division involved in it with no contradictions.

One becomes what one resolves to be, upnishad shows the meditation based on symbol as some name etc. get movement as far as name extend by organ of speech which is greater than name, “he gets freedom as far as speech extend, and, mind being greater then speech and so on, these distinction about result is possible for meditation based on symbol.

However, meditation based on brahman or without symbol leads to brahman only, since no gradation is possible for brahman and brahman being without distinction.</td></tr>
</table>

Section IV

Doubt	Explanation
Having reached highest light, does that being or *atman* is manifested with some distinction like a region of heaven, or it is the self alone	Term used in *upnishad* is "in its own", so the soul or *atman* manifest in its true nature and the difference between earlier state and the final state is self or *atman* becoming free from erstwhile bondage and continues as pure self. Earlier state is becoming blind and tainted by three states (waking, dreaming & sleeping), while liberated soul becomes inseparable from brahman as stated in *upnishad.* Further it is confirmed in *upnishad,* that liberated soul is established in attributes that brahman has (self is beyond sin etc & individual soul is same as supreme self) and liberated soul is established as pure consciousness which is its true nature
Upnisidic text state "should he desire world of manes, it becomes associated with him" is just a wish, as cause of appearance	Manes and other comes as result of wish alone, since for man with knowledge has no other lord Like lamp can appear to be many through its power of transformation (lighting

	other lamp with one) so the man of knowledge though one through its divine power becomes many and enters many bodies to animate them
How can liberated man, have such divine power of entering into many bodies	To the knower of brahman everything becomes self; while falling asleep, he craves no dream and state of divine power is asserted, is the state like heaven which comes with maturity of meditation
One who attains union with God while still having mind can acquire unlimited divine power as result of meditation on qualified brahman	As understood from the context in *upnishad* (dealing with God), released soul gets all the divine power except of running universe (creation, continuance, dissolution) This unlimited power is not an independent sovereignty since God as supreme appoints others to their respective sphere which is at disposal to God alone.